Mille Miglia Race

The
Postwar years

Edited by Andrea Curami

GIORGIO NADA EDITORE

GIORGIO NADA EDITORE S.r.l.

Editorial and production supervisor
Antonio Maffeis

Graphic design
Sergio Nada

Layout
Ufficio Grafico Giorgio Nada Editore

Photographs
Giorgio Nada Editore Archive
Corrado Millanta Archive
Andrea Curami Archive

Colour separations
MENHIR Produzione - S. Egidio alla Vibrata (TE)

Printer
Grafiche D'Auria - Ascoli Piceno

The catalogue of publications of Giorgio Nada Editore
is available at the following address:
Giorgio Nada Editore, via Claudio Treves 15/17,
20090 Vimodrone (MI) - Italy
Tel ++39/02/27301126 - Fax ++39/02/27301454
E-mail: nadamail@sii.it

© 1998 Giorgio Nada Editore, Vimodrone (Milan)
Printed in Italy

Mille Miglia Race
The Postwar years - ISBN 88-7911-188-4

Contents

PIRELLI
sicurezza nella velocità

PNEUMATICI
◄CEAT►

VERIFICA
CATEGORIA TURISMO
INTERNAZIONALE

THE MILLE MIGLIA IN THE YEARS OF POST-WAR RECONSTRUCTION

Last year has seen the seventieth anniversary of the birth of the Mille Miglia and the fiftieth anniversary of the post-war revival of the Brescian race.

We have chosen to celebrate this joint anniversary by allowing our readers to enjoy some of the articles written by the most famous motoring journalists of the era and published in magazines such as Motor Sport, The Autocar and The Motor.

We felt that as a support to these texts our readers would appreciate a pictorial review of most of the cars that won the numerous prizes on offer each year, the details being gathered from the programmes published to accompany the following year's race.

The majority of the photographs come from the Novafoto archive, today owned by Giorgio Nada Editore. Alberto Sorlini, the proprietor of the Novafoto photographic agency of Brescia documented on behalf of the organisers each of the post-war editions of the Mille Miglia, photographing the contestants at the start and finish and along the route.

In order to complement and complete the list of the prize-winning cars we have also drawn on the Millanta archive and our own collection.

Giorgio Nada
Andrea Curami

Motor Sport, August, 1947

THE MILLE MIGLIA

Biondetti's "2.9" unsupercharged Alfa-Romeo wins Italian 1,000 mile race. Cisitalias occupy the next three places.

Biondetti, partnered by Romano, who tuned the car, won this year's Mille Miglia in a 2.9-litre straight-eight Alfa-Romeo coupé with four Solex carburetters. In spite of losing his two lower gears on the first section between Brescia and Rome, Biondetti averaged 69.9 m.p.h. for the 1,125 miles, inclusive of five stops to look to the fuel feed. In all, 245 cars entered for the various classes. Immense enthusiasm greeted the start at Brescia. For a time Gilera's Fiat led, but at Rome Nuvolari was in the lead in a Cisitalia saloon. Known to be a sick man-alas, we have heard this of Tazio too often of late-Nuvolari neverthless drove magnificently, but neither he, nor Carena, his co-driver, could hold off Biondetti. The long, rough course took immense toll of the big field and torrential rain did not improve matters. Taruffi's Cisitalia was out before reaching Rome, Cortese had gasket bothers and retired the new Ferrari after 265 miles, Villoresi was let down by bearing failure in the new sports Maserati, while Dusio was in trouble at Tadino, rain having

played havoc with his Cisitalia's engine. Nuvolari still led after 958 miles, but beyond Asti the long straights gave the far bigger Alfa-Romeo its change and it went ahead. The Cisitalia was further delayed some 15 minutes when Nuvolari had to change a magneto after rain-water had swamped his engine. He finished 15 min. 56 sec. behind Biondetti and was carried to an hotel for medical attention. The other team -Cisitalia driven by Bernabei and Minetti - came in 3rd and 4th on general classification, a horde of 1,100- c.c. Fiat saloons followed them in, driven by Capelli, Della Chiesa, Ermini, Comirato and Balestrero, while in 10th place came Reynaldi's Lancia "Aprilia" saloon, which won the touring-car class at an average of nearly 61 m.p.h. Fastest along the final autostrada was Bernabei's Cisitalia, at 94.8 m.p.h. This great race was possible because the energetic Brescia A.C. was allowed to close over 1,000 miles of public road and because the Minister of Commerce allocated 20,000 gallons of 80 octane fuel and tyres via Pirelli, sufficient for the race.

THE MILLE MIGLIA
Biondetti, Alfa-Romeo, wins in torrential rain

NUVOLARI
CISITALIA
XIV - 1947
22 - CT. TORINO

Held at last after two postponements, the Mille Miglia was won by Biondetti driving an Alfa-Romeo by just over 32 minutes from Nuvolari with an open version of the new 1,100 c.c. sports Cisitalia. Bernabei Cisitalia, was third, and Minetti, Cisitalia, fourth, so that in their first event the new Cisitalias occupied three of the first four positions. From the start at Brescia the 1,125-mile course made for the mountains near Lake Garda, then run south along the Adriatic to Pesaro and across the Appenines to Rome. From Rome the competitors headed north-west to Turin; 145 miles of very fast autostrada brought the weary competitors back to Brescia via Milan. Many critics thought that the course was too long and too rough. Nevertheless, the Brescia A. C. has certainly shown abundant energy in holding the race at all, for the club had to arrange for the closing of over a thousand miles of road, persuade the Minister of Commerce to allocate 20,000 gallons of 80 octane fuel for the event, and arrange for the Pirelli company to provide sufficient tyres. The astonishing total of 245 touring, sports and racing

cars was entered for the event, of which number the only British car was an M.G. Midget driven by Cenacchi.

The enormous field included few works entries. Alfa-Romeo were fully occupied preparing the Alfettes for the Grand Prix of Europe at Spa and did not enter, but sixteen Alfas were being driven in the 3-litre class by private owners, the favourite being Biondetti's 2.9-litre unsupercharged coupé. There were scenes of great enthusiasm at the start at Brescia as the first of a seemingly endless stream of Fiat 500s fitted with all manner of queer streamlined bodies by local enthusiasts left at 8 p.m. last Saturday for Bologna. The

cars were despatched at minute intervals and so large was the entry that the last competitors did not set off until three in the morning.

At Padua, a hundred miles to the south-east, Gilera with a Fiat was leading the general classification at an average speed of 83.1 m.p.h. with two other Fiats lying second and third. Before Pesaro, 250 miles from the start, had been reached, the second man, Bassi, had taken the lead at an average of 72.6 m.p.h., with an Alfa driven by Lanza in second place.

At Rome a well-organized public address system linked with the other controls gave constant news of the progress fo the race

to a vast and enthusiastic crowd. The first car to reach there was Tullini's Lancia Aprilia, which had averaged over 60 m.p.h. for the 446 miles. The leader of the general classification was now Nuvolari, who came into the Rome control only seconds ahead of his team mates, Bernabei and Minetti, and received a tremendous ovation from the excited crowd, which was barely under control.

By this time the fine weather at the start had turned to rain and already many favourites had retired. Cortese and the new Ferrari went out of the race at Fano with gasket trouble after covering 265 miles. His immediate rival, Villoresi, with the

Pre-race scrutineering for the first post-war Gordini 11 Sport, baptised as the "Mille Miles" and entrusted for the occasion to Franco Rol and Nando Righetti, followed by the Cisitalia 202 CMM of Piero Taruffi and Buzzi. Both cars were to retire before reaching Rome.
On the facing page, the Cisitalia 202 of Tazio Nuvolari at the Turin checkpoint. The Mantuan was to complete the race in sparkling style, finishing second overall and first in the Sport 1100 class.

new Maserati, retired with bearings, whilst Pietro Dusio retired after 313. miles at Tadino when driving rain found its way into the engine compartment and caused plug and worse trouble. A second member of the Cisitalia team, Taruffi with the pacemaker, retired before Rome.

Nearly 70 m.p.h. Average

Nuvolari reached Florence still leading the general classification, having covered the 721 miles in 10 hours 13 minutes 13 seconds, an average speed of 69.95 m.p.h. With every reason to be satisfied with such an average in an unblown 1,100 c.c. saloon, Nuvolari handed over the wheel to his co-driver Carena for a spell. But close behind him into Rome came Biondetti, whose average was only fractionally below Nuvolari's. In third place was Minetti with a Cisitalia. At this stage the new Cisitalias were putting up an outstanding fight and were lying first, third and fourth. The worst of the mountain roads lay behind; ahead of them stretched the long Via Emilia to Turin and then finally the fast Autostrada to Milan.
Could Nuvolari, who was known to be a sick man, keep ahead of Biondetti's much larger Alfa?

Until Asti, 958 miles from the start, Nuvolari still led but on the long straight roads of the north his marvellous driving with the small car did not count for so much and the bigger Alfa made up time in spite of having only top and third gears and took the lead. Although now winning, Biondetti never saw Nuvolari, for he started over an hour behind Tazio.
The vast crowds lining the route did not know who was leading, for the electric storms had put the telephone lines between the

controls out of action, but the magic name of Nuvolari thrilled across Italy. The weather grew steadily worse and conditions on the Turin-Milan-Brescia autostrada were indescribable. One competitor, Balestrero, driving a Fiat had to stop beneth a bridge, for a cloudburst made it quite impossible to see the road. The saloons were now at an advantage and at 3 p.m. the first car came into Brescia in a tropical downpour. At the head of the touring car class was Reynaldi's Lancia Aprilia, which

had covered the route in 18 hours 41 minutes 22 seconds at an average speed on nearly 61 m.p.h., and which finished tenth in the general classification. Nuvolari finished in second place at about 4.30 p.m. on Sunday and was so exhausted by more than sixteen hours of driving in what was virtually a small racing car that he had almost to be lifted out of the Cisitalia and carried into an hotel to receive medical attention. The winner, big, burly, modest Biondetti, was in better shape when his Alfa

	Results		
	Driver	Car	Time
1	Biondetti	2.9 litre Alfa-Romeo	16 hr. 16 min. 39sec. (Average 69.9 mph)
2	Nuvolari	1,100 c.c. Cisitalia	16 hr. 32 min. 35 sec.
3	Bernabei	1,100 c.c. Cisitalia	16 hr. 38 min 17 sec.
4	Minetti	1,100 c.c. Cisitalia	17 hr. 0 min. 40 sec.
5	Capelli	1,100 c.c. Fiat	
6	Della Chiesa	1,100 c.c. Fiat	
7	Ermini	1,100 c.c. Fiat	
8	Comirato	1,100 c.c. Fiat	
9	Balestrero	1,100 c.c. Fiat	
10	Reynaldi	1,485 c.c. Lancia	(Editor's note: later disqualified)

*The Alfa Romeo 2900 B Touring (1)
of Emilio Romano and Clemente
Biondetti were first home to Brescia
at an average speed of 111.995 kph.
They also won the 3000 cc Sport
Internazionale class and the
relative class of the F. di M. Grand
Prix on the Turin-Brescia
motorway stage at an average
speed of 142.006 kph.*

coupé rolled to a standstill at the finish after 16 hours 16 minutes and 39 seconds of very hard motoring, an average of just under 70 m.p.h. for the whole course. Biondetti runs a motor business in Florence and his Alfa was not prepared by the works. In fact he wanted to drive a Talbot-Darracq in the race, and Alfas are therefore lucky to have won this event for the tenth time. When interviewed after the race Biondetti said that they had stopped five times with fuel

trouble. His Alfa is a fixed-head coupé and was tuned by Romano, with whom he shared the driving. As blowers were banned the twin superchargers had been replaced by four Solex carburettors and the compression ratio had been raised. The car ran through the whole race on the same set of Pirelli tyres.

Nuvolari said that the mountains were the most difficult part of the course and rain seemed to fall all the time. He lost about fifteen

minutes at the Ticino Bridge diversion on the Turin-Milan autostrada when water swamped the engine and made a magneto change necessary. In spite of the wind and the rain and the parked traffic at the side Nuvolari said that his light open car had not proved difficult to handle on the autostrada.

It is of interest that Bernabei's Cisitalia was the fastest car on the final stretch of autostrada, averaging over 94.8 m.p.h.

Second overall and first in the 1100 Sport Internazionale class was the Cisitalia 202 MM (2) of Tazio Nuvolari and Carena, preceding the Cisitalia 202 "Cassone" berlinetta (3) built by Rocco Motto and driven by Inico Bernabei and Tullio Pacini which won the F. di M. Grand Prix at an average speed of 153,413 kph. In the photo (3), Bernabei's car is followed by the Cisitalia 202 SMM of Eugenio Minetti and Pietro Facetti which finished fourth overall, completing the success of the young Turin marque.

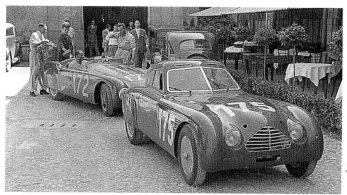

The Fiat 1100 S of Ovidio Capelli-Gerli (4), fifth overall at an average speed of 105. 412 kph, seen here in the torrential rain that accompanied the competitors on the motorway stage. Another photo of the Cisitalia 202 SMM of Minetti-Facetti (race number 172) and the "Cassone" berlinetta of Bernabei-Pacini (5), the first aerodynamic design for the firm by the engineer Savonuzzi.

The 1100 Turismo Internazionale class was won by the Lancia Ardea of Enrico Coda and Dama (seen here at the start of the 1948 edition), at an average speed of 85.716 kph. Diego Capelli and Nosotti took the 750 cc class of the same category with their Fiat 500, whilst Alberto Guardia and Gino Locchi of Verona with another Fiat 500 won their class in the F. di M Grand Prix at almost 89 kph.

1

2

The Lancia Aprilia of Reynaldi and Moroni (1) was the first of the 1500 TI class home to Brescia, but the car was subsequently disqualified following post-race scrutineering. Arnaldo Tullini and Francesco Rossi (2) with their Aprilia were, therefore, promoted to class winners, and in any case won the F. di M. Grand Prix at an average speed of 121.937 kph.
Gino de Sanctis and Posperi (3) won with a Fiat 508C Balilla the 1100 TI class of the F. di M. Grand Prix at the average speed of 102.030 kph. This photo was taken at the start of the 1948 edition.

3

1

2

3

1) The Paganelli Lancia bodied by
Touring (in the background with
race number 185), winner of the
Italian championship in 1939 with
Luigi Bellucci, was driven to
victory by Meschi and Bianchi in
the 2000 cc Sport Internazionale
category and the F. di M. Grand
Prix (average speed: 130.987 kph).
Mario Avalle and Antonio Prina

won the 750 cc SI category with this
Avalle Fiat (2) built to the more
restrictive specifications of the
Sport Nazionale category of which
it was Italian national champion
that season.
3) Antonio Stagnoli and Lucchetta
won their class trophy on the
motorway section with this Fiat 500
special.

MILLE MIGLIA

A Healey Saloon Wins the Touring-Car Category

This year's famous 1,000-Mile Race was very strenuous indeed for what is, in any case, an arduous event, for the roads were for the most part slippery. The early stages of this great contest saw Nuvolari's V12 Ferrari in the lead at 76 m.p.h., but trouble set in and he gave way to his team-mate Cortese, who, however, had lost third-speed of his five-speed gearbox. Cortese, too, retired, but Biondetti, who won last year in an Alfa-Romeo saloon at 69.9 m.p.h., then went into the lead for the team, finally winning at an average speed of 75.84 m.p.h. in his V12, three-carburetter, transverse-leaf, i.f.s., 2-litre Ferrari coupé. His co-driver was Navone, and their fine drive occupied 15 hr. 5min. 44 sec. The winning Ferrari was followed home by a mass of special F.I.A.T.s, the streamlined 1,100-c.c. saloon version handled by Comirato and Dumas and by Apruzzi and his brother being 2nd and 3rd, at average of 69.1 and 67.25 m.p.h., respectively. Four Lancia "Aprilias", two Healeys and a Cisitalia also finished in the first twenty, but Taruffi (Cisitalia), Banti (Cisitalia), and Amendola (Maserati) were amongst the many who retired,

the last-named due to a crash which killed Bai, the co-driver. Ascari and Sanesi also failed to finish, the latter crashing and badly injuring himself. The Healeys from England made a brave show and secured grand prestige thereby. Donald Heaely, partnered by his son, got his two-seater home 9th, in spite of hitting a dog and damaging his car severely, while Count Lurani and Sandri, in a saloon, finished 13th on general classification, in spite of having lost its rear-axle locating rod. Lurani's car made the fastest (and record) average in the touring-car class, winning at 65.15 m.p.h., after a fine run lasting 17 hr. 32 min. 12 sec.. They beat the Lancia "Aprilia" of Borniga and his brother and another car of this make and type, handled by Bracco, these taking 2nd and 3rd places. Capelli and Nosotti in a F.I.A.T. won the under-1,100-c.c. touring-car class.

Of the sports cars, Bianchetti's Alfa-Romeo was fastest of the over-2 litre cars at 66.45 m.p.h., the race-winning Ferrari the 2-litre division, Comirato and Dumas the under 1,100-c.c. category at over 61 m.p.h. in a F.I.A.T., while Fiorio and Avalle's F.I.A.T. 500 took the under-750-c.c. sports-car class.

General Classification:

1st: Biondetti and Navone (2-litre Ferrari), 15 hr. 5 min. 44 sec.

2nd: Comirato and Dumas (1,100-c.c. F.I.A.T.), 16 hr. 33 min. 8 sec.

3rd: Apruzzi and Apruzzi (1,100-c.c. F.I.A.T.), 16 hr. 52 min. 30 sec.

Touring cars up to 1,100 c.c.:

1st: Capelli and Nosotti (1,100-c.c. F.I.A.T.), 20 hr. 5 min. 42 sec.

2nd: Minzoni and Chiti (1,100-c.c. F.I.A.T.), 20 hr. 18 min. 58 sec.

3rd: G. Caffaro and M. Caffaro (1,100-c.c. F.I.A.T.), 20 hr. 21 min. 5 sec.

Sports cars up to 750 c.c.:

1st :   Fiorio and Avalle (F.I.A.T. 500), 19 hr. 37 min. 29 sec.

2nd: Francesconi and Chinellato (F.I.A.T. 500), 20 hr. 23 mi. 36 sec.

3rd: Panzacchi and Faccioli (F.I.A.T. 500), 20 hr. 48 min. 45 sec.

Touring cars over 1,100 c.c.:

1st: Lurani and Sandri (Healey), 17 hr. 32 min. 12 sec.

2nd: Bornigia and Bornigia (Lancia), 17 hr. 47 min. 49 sec.

3rd: Asti and Asti (Lancia), 17 hr. 59 min. 4 sec.

Sports cars up to 1,100 c.c.:

1st: Comirato and Dumas (1,100-c.c. F.I.A.T.), 16 hr. 33 min. 8 sec.

2nd: F. Apruzzi and A. Apruzzi (1,100-c.c. F.I.A.T.), 16 hr. 52 min. 30 sec.

3rd: Terigi and Berti (1,100-c.c. F.I.A.T.), 16 hr. 57 min. 10 sec.

Sports cars up to and over 2 litres classes united:

1st: Biondetti and Navone (Ferrari), 15 hr. 5 min. 44 sec.

2nd: Bianchetti and Cornaggia (Alfa-Romeo), 17 hr. 2 min. 43 sec.

3rd: D. Healey and G. Healey (Healey), 17 hr. 26 min. 10 sec.

A view of the crowded scrutineering paddock in Piazza della Vittoria.
On the facing page, bottom, the start at Brescia with the Healey 2400 "Elliot" driven by the engineer Count Giovanni Lurani Cernuschi and the motorcycle champion Guglielmo Sandri.

THE MILLE MIGLIA

New 2-litre Ferrari Wins Italy's Greatest Sports Car Race: Meritorious Performance by British Healey Driven by Donald Healey and Count Lurani

Two comparatively new makes of car, using motor racing to establish their reputations, succeeded last week-end when the fifteenth Mille Miglia was run off over slightly more than 1,000 miles of Italy's main roads.

The race was won outright by a coupé-bodied 2-litre unsupercharged Ferrari, made in Modena, Italy, and driven by that fine and veteran Italian driver Clemente Biondetti, who has twice won the race before. Following this result, which is called the general classification of the race, there is the touring category and it is pleasant to be able to record that this proved a victory, for the first time, for a British car, the 2-litre Healey saloon driven by Count Lurani, the same car which won its class in the recent Tour of Sicily. The latter event was described by Lurani in a special article last week, and it is hoped to include a further edition of his personal experiences in the Mille Miglia in an early issue. Last week-end he changed his spare driver and was accompanied by Sandri. Several Healeys had been entered for the race but only three competed, those driven by Lurani, by Donald Healey himself, and by Haines, the Healey agent from Belgium. Donald Healey did very well to finish as high as ninth in the general classification. Lurani being thirteenth. The vast majority of the starters, which numbered well over one hundred, were Fiats, and this make was second and third in the general classification with streamlined saloons of only 1,100 c.c., an exceptional performance.

The Mille Miglia is an extremely confusing race to follow because, as explained in the special article last week ("A High-Speed Rally"), when nearly 200 cars set off over 1,000 miles right across Italy and have to make time checks at various points, the event as a whole becomes more likes a high-speed rally. Thus the first car actually to finish at Brescia was Lurani's Healey but he was not, of course, the race winner. There not been a massed start, cars leaving Brescia on Saturday night at short intervals and returning to Brescia on Sunday afternoon in very scattered groups, after anything between fifteen and nearly twenty hours' driving.

But the winning average of some 75 m.p.h. over this great distance shows that the Mille Miglia is certainly run at racing speeds and that to the driver it is one of the most formidable events in which he can partake. This year the pace set in the opening stages was in fact so hot that most of the favourites dropped out before half distance.

Thus Ferrari, who were obviously making the fullest efforts this year, had obtained as drivers the aces Nuvolari and Cortese, besides Biondetti. Nuvolari set his usual cracking pace, averaging at one time 80 m.p.h., and -sacrificing all comfort to speed - had jettisoned much equipment. But when in the lead his Ferrari developed trouble and he was forced to retire, having averaged till then 76 m.p.h.

Cortese had lost third gear by the time he reached Rome, the most southerly point of the course, but continued, helped doubtless by the fact that his car had a five-speed gear box anyway, but he, too, had to give up at Bologna on the northerly run home. Biondetti continued -he had been twenty-three minutes behind Nuvolari- to win.

Of the Cisitalia, another post-war make, which had finished second, third and fourth last year, Taruffi and Banti had to retire just short of Rome. Other well-known drivers who retired included Ascari and Sanesi, the latter being involved in a crash and receiving injuries. Inevitably in the bad weather, with slippery roads over the mountains and the uncertain conditions of traffic which can hardly be effectively shut out of so long a distance,

there were other crashes and Amendola's Maserati went off the road, the second driver, Bai, being killed.

Naturally it must be some time before the result of such a vast event can be properly collated and judged. The timing system in itself is complex, there are usually protests to be dealt with - especially as to whether cars really complied with the touring category regulations - and it is difficult to ascertain the exact reasons for failures. And so there has been in the daily press - rightly elated at the British successes- a certain amount of variation in the reports, which can be understood in the circumstances. But although Lurani's win in the touring category must not be confused or compared with Biondetti's victory in the race proper, it is

none the less an historic achievement for the new British make from Warwick. Any car which goes the whole distance at a respectable average in the Mille Miglia must be a good car, and it usually takes an Italian driver who knows more than most about the huge course to get the best out of a particular car. The more credit, then, to Donald Healey, who can hardly have had the opportunity for any practice at all, for finishing so high in the final race list.

Out of the first twenty cars to be placed in that general classification there were the winning Ferrari, ten Fiats, six Lancia Aprilias, the two Healeys and one Cisitalia. And doubtless all of those had their own troubles and adventurers even thoufh they were more successful than most. Lurani's car, for instance, again

broke the locating rod for the rear axle which had given trouble in Sicily, and Healeys' own machine is said to have hit a dog at high speed, damaging the front of the car.

The successful Ferrari is in design one of the most advanced sporting cars in the world. It has a V-twelve-cylinder engine, with three carburettors mounted between the cylinder blocks, and fitted into a tubular frame with transverse leaf spring independent front-wheel suspension.

A saloon is often at an advantage in the modern Mille Miglia because the final run of some 150 miles is along the Turin-Milan-Brescia autostrada, and there, where speeds in the neighbourhood of 100 m.p.h. are averaged, the most efficient streamlining may count. Thus last year Biondetti also decided to drive a saloon, an Alfa-Romeo, and in that race again the coupé Cisitalias were faster than the open cars of the same make. Healey himself found that he averaged some 90 m.p.h. for more than 100 miles.

Out of all those cars to start from Brescia slightly over sixty manged to finish.

The Ferrari 166 S berlinetta bodied by Allemano (1) of Clemente Biondetti and Giuseppe Navone triumphed in this edition, winning overall at an average speed of 121.227 kph, and taking the 2000 cc SI class and the Grand Prix F. di M. at an average of 157. 381 kph. Alberto Comirato, with his wife Lia Dumas, finished second overall and first in the 1100 SI class in this Comirato Fiat (2) with a Gilco tubular frame and an engine derived from the 1100 S.

1

2

The Francesco Apruzzi-Angelo Apruzzi pairing finished third overall with the Fiat 1100 S (3), and won the special class reserved for 1100 cc closed sports cars, ahead of Guido Scagliarini and the Fiat 1100 S of Christillin-Nasi. At the wheel of this Stanguellini 1100 (4), bodied by Ala d'Oro of Reggio Emilia, Aldo Tergi and Berti finished fourth overall at an average speed of 107.946 kph.

3

1

Guido Scagliarini, accompanied by
Maffiodo, finished fifth overall with
this Cisitalia 202 coupé corsa (1),
also winning the Alberani Cup for
the best time recorded on the
Raticosa Pass. In 1948 Scagliarini
won the Italian national class
championship. Sandro Fiorio,
along with Piero Avalle, finished
first in the 750 Sport class, driving
this old 1940 model Siata 750
skilfully modified by the Avati
brothers.
The over 2-litre Sport class was won
by Giampiero Bianchetti and Gian
Maria Cornaggia Medici at the
wheel of this Alfa Romeo 2500 SS
modified by Canavesi and bodied
by Colli (3).

2

3

1) Giovanni Lurani Cernuschi (Healey), paired with the motorcycle champion Guglielmo Sandri, won the over 1100 cc Turismo Internazionale class at an average speed of over 104 kph. The aristocratic.Milan engineer also won the Italian national class championship that year. Diego Capelli and Veronelli won their class with the Fiat 1100, and also won the Italian 1100 cc championship title at the end of the season.

Gino Locchi and Ubaldo Zunica of Verona (Fiat 500), won the special class reserved for 750 cc touring cars. Bosini and Facca, at the wheel of this 750 sport of Fiat derivation (2) won the cup awarded to the leading team from Brescia in the 750 Sport class by the Brescia car club and the Associazione Fratelli d'Italia. This photo was taken during the 1950 edition.
Giovanni Bracco and Umberto Magioli (Lancia Aprilia Turismo Internazionale) won the Agnelli Cup for the highest placed team on the Tour of Sicily and Mille Miglia events. Remy Jacazio (driving a Lancia Aprilia Sport with Enrico Anselmi) won the cup offered to the first journalist home.

HEALEY TRIUMPHS IN MILLE MIGLIA

Beats All Comers in Touring-car Class

This year's 26th Mille Miglia (Thousand Miles Race), run on Sunday, April 24, provided terrific fights in both the sports and touring car classes from start to finish of the exhausting 993-mile course which starts at Brescia in Lombardy and runs round half Italy.

British cars were entered in the touring class-Count Lurani and H.J. Aldington with the Bristol which did so well in the recent and similar Targa Florio, and Healeys driven by Donald Healey himself, and another by Tommy Wisdom and Donald's son, both saloon models.

The cars are sent off one by one at intervals and from then there was a quadripartite battle between Sanesi and Venturi (Alfa-Romeo), the Wisdom-Healey car and the Lurani-Aldington Bristol, with Donald Healey close up. This struggle was fought out all day, the cars dashing into the controls on each other's heels. Enormous crowds packed the towns and villages and lined the country roads in glorious weather and cheered the British cars as they flashed past. At the finish only four minutes covered the first three. Wisdom and Healey, Junr., made a last magnificent effort and tore across the finishing line back at Brescia 1 min. 54 secs. ahead of

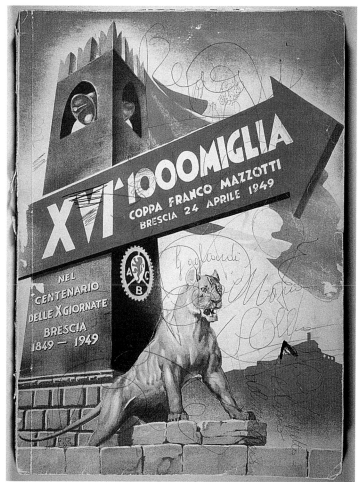

the Alfa, which shook the dense crowds not a little. Aldington and Lurani (Bristol) came in only 4 mins. 2 secs. later, and in fourth place Donald Healey came home 26 mins. later.

Running in this Touring class was another Healey driven by British drivers Cohen and Hignett, but the car crashed 16 miles after the start. in the darkness of the small hours, and it is reported that both drivers were fatally injured.

Following the British demonstration in the Targa Florio, this pratical domination of the touring car class of the most gruelling of all races cannot but create a profound impression.

In the sports class the race opened with a grim duel between Taruffi and Bonetto, both on 2-litre Ferraris, pursued by Roll (Alfa Romeo). Biondetti (Ferrari) and Cortese (Ferrari). Taruffi blew up, Bonetto slowed, and Biondetti snatched the lead and kept it to the finish. The Serafini-Haller Frazer-Nash also gave up. Another Type 120 Frazer-Nash was entered by Tenbosch and P.R. Monkhouse, and a third, driven by Calpin, crashed on its way out to Italy.

Luigi Fagioli competed with this Fiat 1100 S, here seen having its race number painted, and finished sixth in class and eleventh overall at Brescia.

There was an immense field of 302 starters and it is not perhaps suprising that among so many who must be inexperienced drivers, there were many crashes, some serious.

The course ran from Brescia southwest to Piacenza; thence to Parma, Apuania on the Mediterranea coast, and along the coast southwards to the outskirts of Rome. From here the way led north-east to Terni, over the mountains to Pescara on the Adriatic, up the coast through Ancona to Ravenna, thence to Ferrara and Padua and due west back through Verona to Brescia. The circuit for the Mille Miglia has been changed frequently with the passing years. In 1948, for instance, it ran in a clockwise direction, which was the opposite of the traditional.

This year the race was sliced into two separate but equal sections -(a) sports cars, (b) touring cars - each of which was subdivided into engine-size categories. Sports cars had to be listed models, but could be tuned in the ordinary way and run on high-octane fuels. Touring cars could not be altered in any particular and had to run on "pump" fuel. Superchargers were banned in both classes. No British car has yet won the Mille Miglia outright-indeed, the list of victors has been completely dominated by Alfa Romeo - but in 1933 and M.G. Magnette driven by Count Lurani and George Eyston won the 1,100 c.c. class, and in the following year Lurani and Penn-Hughes ran second in the class, again with an M.G. Magnette. In 1935 an Aston Martin T.T.-type car won the 1.500 c.c. class, driven by Tommy Clarke and Maurice Faulkner. British cars reappeared in the race last year, when Count Lurani and Sandri on a Healey saloon won the over-1,100 c.c. touring class and were 13th irrespective of category. Donald Healey and his son also drove a Healey that year in the sports class and finished ninth after smiting a dog and smashing their head lamps.

1) The home-built Furia of Attilio Guelfi and Mario Repetto at pre-race scrutineering.
The car was a hybrid based on a Fiat 1100 chassis with a DKW engine of almost two litres capacity. The team retired between Parma and Livorno.
2) The OSCA 1100 of Franco Cornacchia-Lesma, the only example of the marque to start the race, was to retire before Pescara when lying eleventh overall and fourth in class.

3) Enzo Ferrari in conversation with the engineer Giovanni Canestrini during the pre-race scrutineering.

MILLE MIGLIA PLACINGS

Placings in the Mille Miglia 1,000-Mile Sports Car Race, which was won by Biondetti and Salani in a 2-litre Ferrari, are given below. Britain was well up, for Wisdom and young Geoffrey Healey won the touring category outright in a Healey, while the Bristol saloon of Count Lurani and H.J. Aldington was third and Donald Healey's Healey saloon fourth in this class. Retirements included Taruffi (Ferrari) with engine failure after clocking 130 m.p.h. over a timed kilometre, Gordon and Lewis (Lancia Astura). Cohen and Hignett (Healey) who crashed at Manerbio with fatal results to the latter, and Serafini and Haller (Type 120 Frazer-Nash).

General Classification:
1st: Biondetti and Salani (2,000-c.c. Ferrari), 12 hr. 7 min. 5 sec., 81.687 m.p.h.
2nd: Bonetto and Carpani (2,000-c.c. Ferrari), 12 hr. 35 min. 7 sec.
3rd: Rol and Richiero (2,443-c.c. Alfa-Romeo) 12 hr. 51 min. 10 sec.

Over 2,000 c.c.:
1st: Rol and Richiero (2,443-c.c. Alfa-Romeo), 12 hr. 51 min. 10 sec., 77.035 m.p.h.
2nd: S. Basso and L. Basso (2,443-c.c. Alfa-Romeo), 15 hr. 51 min. 46 sec.

2,000 c.c.:
1st: Biondetti and Salani (2,000-c.c. Ferrari), 12 hr. 7 min. 5 sec. 81.687 m.p.h.
2nd: Bonetto and Carpani (2,000-c.c. Ferrari), 12 hr. 35 min. 7 sec.

1,100 c.c.:
1st: Auricchio and Bozzini (1,100-c.c. F.I.A.T.), 13 hr. 57 min. 52 sec., 71.106 m.p.h.
2nd: Scagliarini and Maggio (Cisitalia), 14 hr. 9 min. 42 sec.

750 cc.:
1st: Magiorelli and Maggiorelli (F.I.A.T. Special) 16 hr. 53 min. 30 sec., 58.601 m.p.h.
2nd: Paesetti and Lana, 17 hr. 3 min. 3 sec.

Touring Category
Over 1,100 c.c.:
1st: G. Healey and T. Wisdom (2,443-c.c. Healey) 14 hr. 24 min. 3 sec.; 68.738 m.p.h.
2nd: Venturi and Sanesi (2,443c.c. Alfa-Romeo), 14 hr. 25 min. 57 sec.
3rd: G. Lurani and HH.J. Aldington (1,971-c.c. Bristol), 14 hr. 28 min. 5 sec.
4th: D. Healey and G. Price (2,443-c.c. Healey), 14 hr. 50 min. 50 sec.

1,100 c.c.:
1st: Segré and Valenzano (1,100-c.c. F.I.A.T.), 16 hr. 34 min. 12 sec., 59.703 m.p.h.
2nd: Mariani and Mariani (1,100-c.c. F.I.A.T.), 16 hr. 41 min. 32 sec.

750 c.c.:
1st: Ferraguti and Ferraiolo (500-c.c. F.I.A.T.), 18 hr. 47 min. 6 sec., 52.96 m.p.h.
2nd: Zanetti and Zunica (500-c.c. F.I.A.T.), 18 hr. 50 min. 12 sec.

4) Clemente Biondetti won the Mille Miglia for the fourth time and is seen here tackling the Piantonia "steps" with his Ferrari 166 MM. The great Tuscan driver also won the Roseto degli Abruzzi flying kilometre at an average speed of 209.302 kph. He was partnered by Ettore Salani.

1) The Ferrari 166 MM of Felice Bonetto and Ettore Carpani at the start. The pair finished second overall, winning their class on the Parma-Poggio di Berceto leg at an average speed of 99.750 kph.
2) The Alfa Romeo 6C 2500 Competizione of Franco Rol and Richiero, third overall and first in the over 2000 cc Sport Internazionale class.
3) The Fiat 1100 S of Vincenzo Auricchio and Piero Bozzini, fourth overall and first in the crowded 1100 SI class.
4) Guido Scagliarini and Maggio finished fourth overall with this Cisitalia Abarth 204, winning their class on the Parma-Poggio di Berceto leg. At the end of the year Scagliarini emerged as Italian champion in the 1100 Sport Internazionale class.

Among the cars in the Turismo category, the Fiat 500 B of Sergio Ferraguti and Ferraiolo won the 750 cc class at an average speed of 84.701 kph, but was overtaken in the special Parma-Poggio di Berceto classification by the twin car driven by Cavellini-Serina. The 1100 cc class was won by Luigi Segre and Gino Valenzano with this Fiat Monviso cabriolet (1), homologated as a touring car thanks to liberal regulations of the era. The largest class in this category was won by the Healey spider of Geoffrey Healey and Donald Wisdom (2) at an average speed of 110.618 kph. The Fiat 1100 B of Franco Bordoni Bisleri and Eliseo Volpi (3) finished second in class, beating Segre and Valenzano on the Parma-Berceto leg, and the Alfa Romeo 2500 (4) of Franco Venturi, Alfa's Rome concessionaire, and Consalvo Sanesi won the class prize at both Parma and on the Brescia-Chieti section and followed the Healey home by just 53 seconds.

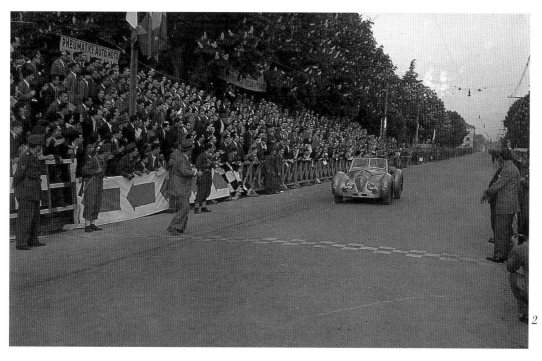

In the Sport Internazionale category, victory in the 750 cc class went to the Benedetti Giannini (1) of the Tuscan pairing M. and A. Maggiorelli at an average speed of 94.306 kph, whilst the Faccioli Fiat (2) of Sanmarco and Boldrini won at Parma and the special classification on the Brescia-Chieti stage. The Fiat 750 derived car (3) of Ito Prati and Pea set the class record on the Roseto degli Abruzzi flying kilometre at an average speed of 143.420 kph. The Stanguellini Ala d'oro 1100 (4) of Montanari and Montanari finished first in class at Chieti, whilst Alberto Comirato with the Comirato Fiat 1100 (5) was the fastest over the flying kilometre, reaching 178,217 kph.

The Ferrari 166 MM of Piero Taruffi and Sergio Nicolini (6) finished first at Giulianova, whilst the unusual AMP (7), built by Placido Prete of Rome and driven Giovanni Rocco and Sorrentino won the over 2000 cc Sport class on the Parma-Berceto leg.

DESPERATE ONE THOUSAND

Ferrari (Marzotto) wins Mille Miglia after appalling weather causes many accidents

Brescia, Monday, April 24.

The seventeenth Mille Miglia held last Sunday saw the record total of 383 cars in sports, touring and standards categories pass the scrutineers. It was one of the most difficult races ever held. Torrential rain and hail, mist and slippery roads, darkness and heavy traffic, wore down the nerves and the stamina of drivers and there were many accidents, some fatal. The first car started at midnight on Saturday, but it was the early hours of Monday morning before the stragglers arrived back at Brescia. The difficulty of policing the long route over this period of time is obvious, and some reduction in entries seems essential if the dangers are to be reduced to reasonable proportions.

The race was a great triumph for private owner Giannini Marzotto, second of a family of four racing brothers, all of whom drove Ferraris. Giannini has been successful in touring events with a Lancia Aprilia, but driving his new Ferrari Superleggera coupé, which was seen at the Geneva Show, with the engine modified to give 2,340 c.c., he pitted his skill against such racing stars as Ascari, Villoresi, Fangio, Biondetti and Serafini, and scored a brillant victory at a speed of 76.562 m.p.h., despite the awful conditions. Marzotto's car was one of several modified to bring them into the unlimited category, but the drivers found themselves confronted by works cars, driven by such formidable opponents as Ascari and Villoresi, with a new 3-3 litre engine. Alfa-Romeo were strongly represented by Juan Fangio, Rol and Bonetto with special short-chassis coupés which have swing axles and transverse springs at the rear. One of these, in the hands of Sanesi, had a new experimental 3-litre engine. Biondetti, four times winner, had chosen an XK 120 Jaguar which was lightened and, incongruously but usefully, fitted with radio in order to receive race bulletins en route.

Other XKs were driven by Leslie Johnson, T.H. Wisdom and Anthony Hume. Nick Haines and Haller, and two Swiss drivers, Ideb and Gaboardi. The Silverstone Healey with Nash engine giving 138 b.h.p. was in the hands of Donald Healey, and Silverstones with the normal engines were driven by P.A. Wood and Peter Monkhouse, Robin Richards and Rodney Lord. The ex-Hichens Aston Martin was handled by Stapleton and Prince Ruffo.

The 2-litre sports class was dominated by Ferraris and Maseratis, while the 750 and 1,100 c.c. sports classes produced a wonderful array of fast specials, in the designing of which Italian engineers are the undisputed masters. The 1,100 c.c. Abarths were challenged by the new twin-camshaft Oscas, one of which was driven privately by Fagioli, middle-aged veteran of pre-war Grand Prix racing, to win the 1,100 c.c. class. Strong competition came from the group of Erminis, which have tubular chassis and four-cylinder twin-camshaft engines said to achieve 10.000 r.p.m., also the latest Stanguellinis, also with four-cylinder twin-overhead camshaft engines.

Potent Small Cars

The National Touring category constituted a private race between Fiat 500s, 1,100s, and Lancia Aprilias, which again achieved astonishing averages. The International Grand Touring category, severely reduced by new regulations, was a fairly easy win

The "patron" Renzo Castagneto and Gigi Villoresi smile for the photographer Alberto Sorlini.

for Schwelm, the Argentine driver, with a Super-leggera Alfa coupé. Three Jaguars had cabriolet tops but failed to qualify in this category as they were ten centimetres under the minimum dimension from pedal to rear axle. Healey saloons and tourers also were not eligible, being one inch under the minimum body width.

Weather forecasts before the start were gloomy, but drivers cheered up when Saturday night broke clear with a bright moon and stars. The touring and small sports cars had a clear run over the first section during the small hours, but mist arrived later, and as dawn broke and the fatest cars approached the starting line, a deluge descended and turned the first 150 miles of road into a skating rink which provoked a series of disastrous crashes. Car after car rocketed away from the starting line as though competing in a Grand Prix, and several small cars went off the road early in, without serious damage to crews; but within a few miles of the start Bassi, the Brescia champion, lost control of his Ferrari at a bridge and crashed. He died soon afterwards, but his mechanic was not dangerously hurt. At 15 kilometres from Padua, Prince Lanza, one of the organizers of the Targa Florio, skidded on another bridge, somersaulted over the embankment,

and rolled over several times in his Cisitalia coupé; miraculously, he escaped with only a cut arm, and his co-driver with a cut head. The car was towed back to the road and driven back to Brescia. Before they got away, however, Wood, driving in his first Mille Miglia, had crashed his Healey at the same spot; he broke a leg and Monkhouse, his co-driver, was thrown against a hoarding carrying, ironically, the words "Good Luck" in English. He was fatally injured. Richards, still under

treatment after breaking both legs, ditched his Healey soon afterwards and broke one leg again, but Lord, his co-driver, was unhurt. Sanesi had crashed his 3-litre Alfa at the same spot minutes before.

Battlefield

One driver said that the countryside was "littered with Ferraris". Umberto Marzotto shattered his 2-litre against a tree, without serious damage to crew, and his brother Paolo ran off the road. Al-

fa-Romeo had suffered a severe setback when Sanesi crashed. He damaged an arm and mechanic Bianchi broke a collarbone. The French D.B., driven by René Simone and De Marco, hit some level crossing gates, and Pizzo Ronconi (Fiat) hit a tree near by. Amid this chaos of crashing cars G. Marzotto took the lead, driving his blue coupé comfortably in a faultless lounge suit. At Ravenna control, 118 miles from the start, he had 2-5 min lead on Villoresi with the new 3.3 litre Fer-

Race distance:

1,682.5 kilometres (1.045.5 miles).

General Classification:

Ferrari 2.340 (Giannino Marzotto: Crosara) 13 hours 39 minutes 20 seconds, 76.562 m.p.h.

Ferrari 2,340 (Serafini : Salani) 13h 46m 53s

Alfa-Romeo 2,443 (Fangio : Zanardi) 14h 2m 5s

Ferrari 2,000 (Bracco : Maglioli) 14h 7m 23.6s

Jaguar 3,442 (Johnson : Lea) 14h 29m 27s

Frazer-Nash 1,971 (Cortese : Ferravazzi) 14h 33m 59s

Osca 1,100 (Fagioli : Diotallevi) 14h 34m 44,4s

Jaguar 3,442 (Biondetti : Manzoni) 14h 38m 39.8s

Ferrari 2,340 (Vittorio Marzotto : Fontana) 14h 39m 2.6s

Alfa-Romeo 2,443 (Schwelm : de Simone) 14h 45m 51.2s

Over 2,000 c.c. Sports

Ferrari (Marzotto G. : Crosara) 13h 39m 20s, 76,56 m.p.h.

Ferrari (Serafini : Salani) 13h 46m 53s

2,000 c.c. Sports

Ferrari (Bracco : Maglioli) 14h 7m 23.3s, 74.03 m.p.h.

Frazer-Nash (Cortese : Ferravazzi) 14h 33m 59s

1,100 c.c. Sports

Osca (Fagioli : Diotallevi) 14h 34 m 44.4s, 71.71 m.p.h.

Fiat (Montanari : Filangeri) 14h 51m 47.2s

750 c.c. Sports

Fiat Patriarca (Leonardi : Prosperi) 15th 55m 40s, 65.73 m.p.h.

Fiat Giannini (Stanga : Stanga) 16h 11m 27s

1,100 c.c. Touring

Fiat (Mancini : Renzi) 17h 8m 29.8s, 60.99 m.p.h.

Fiat (Segre : Valenzano) 17h 12m 48s

International Grand Touring

Alfa-Romeo (Schwelm : de Simone) 14h 45m 51.2s, 70.81 m.p.h.

Alfa-Romeo (Amendola : Pinzero) 15h 35m 40.2s

Over 1,100 c.c. Touring

Alfa-Romeo (Cornaggia : Mantegazza 15h 48m 37s, 66.13 m.p.h.

Lancia Aprilia (Perobelli : Cremonesi) 15h 50m 34.8s

750 c.c. Touring

Fiat 500 (Piodi : Citterio) 18h 43m 57s, 55.82 m.p.h.

Fiat 500 (Castellarin : Coffaccioli) 19h 7m 11s

rari, and had averaged 88 m.p.h. - a wonderful achievement. Next came Serafini with the open 2,340 c.c. Ferrari, and Bonetto with the 4 litre V12 Alfa, an ex Grand Prix car built to the 750 Kilogramme formula, but with blowers removed and   two-seater body fitted. Biondetti (Jaguar) was seventh on time ealapsed and Haller, also with a Jaguar, was holding tenth place. Meanwhile fleeing ahead was the flock of small touring cars led by the standard Fiat 500 coupé of Piodi and Citterio, which averaged an astonishing 62 m.p.h. to Ravenna. A Fiat 1,100, driven by Marin and Golfetto, was maintaining 66.

News of further crashes continued to arrive and Squarcina reported a fractured shoulder after an incident in a Fiat 1,100. Fortunately the weather was clear over the Adriatic and the sea sparkled in bright sunshine as the cars hurtled down the fast coast road. Averages went up rapidly and Villoresi was able to use his extra power to take the lead. By Pescara he had averaged 92 m.p.h. for 375 miles. But Marzotto, unperturbed, was still in second place in the general classification.

Bernabei was out of the race with the 2-litre Ferrari, but Serafini, with the 2,340 c.c. car, was successfully holding off Ascari, with the 3.3 engine, who was throwing treads off tyres at speed. Bracco and Maglioli, and Stagnoli and Bianchi, in Ferraris, were leading the 2-litre class, with Cortese (Frazer-Nash) third. As usual, tremendous speeds by 750 and 1,100 c.c. sports cars challenged the slower cars in the larger categories; Bordini and Da Grada, in the 750 c.c. Da Grada, averaged over 71 m.p.h. to Pescara, and Sighinolfi and Gambarani, in a Stanguellini Fiat 1,100, averaged 81.

The rough and tortuous section across the Appenines to Rome pulled the averages down again and mechanical troubles were by now developing on the faster cars. Ascari and Villoresi both discovered that the new Ferrari engines were too powerful for their chassis and retired with broken transmissions. Leslie Johnson's screenwiper had failed and he drove two-thirds of the race propped up to see over the screen whenever rain fell, which was frequently. The brakes failed on Rol's Alfa-Romeo coupé at a down-hill corner and the car ran up a grass bank as high as a house, without injury to the driver.

Weather was clear at Rome but the light was fading for the faster cars, and by Leghorn they were

1) The changing of the guard: the rising star Juan Manuel Fangio who finished third overall, talking to Tazio Nuvolari.
2) Gigi Villoresi examining the cake depicting the poster for the 1950 edition of the Mille Miglia baked for the traditional reception held in honour of the participants in the race. Overleaf, the Nash-Healey (above) of Donald and Geoffrey Healey and the works Jaguar XK 120 of Haines-Haller.

other competitors, and several drivers were injured in the multiple crash. At Bologna it was a dark and wet night, but thick crowds lined the streets. In Modena, where there is a sharp left turn in the centre of the town, a bugle warned the crowd to clear the road as cars approached. Wisdom, who had entered a Jaguar at the last moment, had been delayed, first by a loose wheel and then by a sticking throttle. He missed the corner at Modena and took the escape road, but Haines, who was following, hesitated and was lost; he crashed into a wall. Wisdom was finally put out by a transmission failure only about 30 miles from the finish. At 6.28 p.m. Leonardi and Prosperi (Fiat 500) crossed the finishing line in Brescia. This was the first time that a baby car had got right round the course without being overtaken by one of the fastest cars and the fact reflects the great length of the entry, with the most powerful cars starting over seven hours after the leaders. Marzotto was not in until nine o'clock, but large crowds were still braving the downpour in Brescia at midnight on Sunday. On Monday 213 cars were reported to have completed the course, and they included the Healey Silverstone driven by the Italians Mostel and Castelbarco.

missed the route at Pisa, but returned and eventually finished.

Limping Home

Biondetti's Jaguar broke a rear spring but the mechanic patched it up and the car continued to finish after a delay of about 40 minutes.

At Leghorn control Jaguars were running five, six, seven, eight and nine in the unlimited sports class. Cortese (Frazer-Nash) was now second to Bracco (Ferrari) in the 2-litre sports class, and Fagioli was making up time on Sighinolfi for the lead in the 1,100 c.c. sports class. The lead in the over-1,100 c.c. touring category was now held by the Lancia Aprilia of Perobelli and Cremonesi, at 69.5 m.p.h., 21 minutes ahead of the next car in the class. Rain and the head lights of approaching traffic were serious hazards to competitors on the Futa and Raticosa passes, and some drivers of open cars were almost stunned by enormous hailstones at one point. The sports Fiat of De Sanctis hit a bridge and spun in front of

using lights. At the Rome control Marzotto was a minute in hand over Serafini, and Fangio was driving grimly to hold third place. Ten minutes behind, Cortese had got the Frazer-Nash two minutes ahead of the leading Jaguar driven by Johnson. The Haines-Haller Jaguar was in ninth place and another XK Jaguar, driven by Gaboardi, was running twelfth in the general classification. Donald and Geoffrey Healey lost time when they were forced off the road by a truck, but the car was lifted back to the road by a helpful group of priests and continued. Unfortunately the control for the overdrive had been smashed and the drivers were obliged to continue running the Nash engine continuously at 5,000 r.p.m. They were now very late and, to add to their troubles,

FERRARI WINS THE MILLE MIGLIA

At the end of April, Italy ran her famous 1,000-mile Brescia-Brescia sports and touring car race under dreadful weather conditions.

There was a record field of 383 and of them all, Giannini Marzotto's Ferrari, with its V12 engine enlarged to 2,340 c.c., and a Superleggera coupé body, gained a convincing victory at 76.57 m.p.h. Ferrari themselves had put in Ascari and Villoresi in the new 3-litre Ferraris and Alfa-Romeo were running their 2 1/2-litre cars in special short-chassis coupé form with swing-axle i.r.s. They were driven by Fangio, Rol and Bonetto, backed up by Sanesi's car with experimental 3-litre engine.

Biondetti, who had won this race four times previously, had an XK 120 Jaguar and Britain was further represented by the XK 120s of Johnson, Wisdom and Hume, Haines and Haller, and Ideb and Gaboardi, and the Healey "Silverstones" of Healey, Wood and Monkhouse, Richards and Lord, and by the pre-war Aston-Martin of Staple-ton and Ruffo. Healey's car had a Nash engine.

The road were extremely slippery and very soon Prince Lanza's Cisitalia coupé had rolled down an embankment, the occupants escaping with minor injuries. Before the car had been towed away, Wood crashed at the same spot, and his co-driver, Peter Monkhouse, sustained fatal head injuries, Wood a broken leg. Richards ditched his Heaely and broke a leg and Sanesi crashed at the same place, damaging his arm. Crashes dominated the race, but Marzotto's Ferrari was away in front, leading Villoresi and Serafini. The best placed British car was Biondetti's Jaguar, running seventh.

Later Villoresi's bigger engine enabled him to overtake Marzotto, and for the first 375 miles he averaged 92 m.p.h. Serafini 2,340-c.c. Ferrari was third, Ascari's 3-litre, troubled by losing tyre treads, fourth. Then the new Ferrari engines broke up the transmission and Rol's brakes failed at an awkward spot. Healey left the road and lost the overdrive gear of the Nash-Healey. Fangio had his Alfa-Romeo up to third place, ahead of Cortese's Frazer-Nash, followed by five Jaguars, in spite of the fact that Johnson's screen-wiper had packed up and Biondetti had been delayed over half an hour by a broken back spring. Later Wisdom's Jaguar, which had been delayed by a loose wheel and sticking throttle, retired with transmission trouble. Haines' Jaguar hit a wall. So British hopes faded and the best our cars could do was fifth, by Johnson's Jaguar. Ferraris were first and second. Alfa-Rorneo third and a Ferrari fourth, but a British Frazer-Nash was second to Bracco's Ferraris in the 2-litre sports-car class. One of the new twin o.h.c. Oscas driven by Fagioli won the 1,100-c.c. sports class, and was as high as seventh in the general classification. F.I.A.Ts dominated all the other classes not won by Ferrari except for an Alfa-Romeo victory in the international Grand Touring category and in the over 1,100-c.c. touring-car class, in which a Lancia Aprilia was second.

1

The arrival of the
Touring bodied
Ferrari 195 S (1)
of Giannino Mar-
zotto and Marco
Crosara, unex-
pected winners of
the race at an av-
erage speed of
123.209 kph. The
wool tycoon's
domination was
undisputed as he
led through all
the time checks
except the one at
Pescara where he
was preceded by
just 6 seconds by
the Ferrari 275 S
of Villoresi and
Pasquale Cas-
sani.

2

JWK 651

Dorino Serafini and Ettore Salani were penalised by the bad weather in their Touring-bodied Ferrari 195 S barchetta (3), finishing second overall, but over seven minutes adrift. The Ferrari 166 MM (4) of Giovanni Bracco and Umberto Maglioli finished fourth overall, winning the 2000 cc Sport Internazionale class, and was just five minutes behind the Alfa Romeo 6C 2500 Competizione (5), entrusted for this edition to Juan Manuel Fangio and Augusto Zanardi, third overall at the Brescia finish.

3

5

4

2) The works Jaguar XK 120 also put up a good showing in the hands of Leslie Johnson and Lea, finishing fifth overall.

In the smallest capacity class of the Turismo category, victory went to the Fiat 500 B of Citterio-Piodi (1) who crossed the finishing line at Brescia after 18 hours, 43' and 47", covering the 1,682 kilometres at an average speed of 89.830 kph. Mancini and Renzi (2) won the 1100 cc class, but were subsequently disqualified at post-race scrutineering and victory went to the Fiat 1100 of Luigi Segre and Gino Valenzano (3) who thus repeated their success of the previous year.

2

1

3

In the over 1100 cc Turismo class, victory went to the Alfa Romeo 2500 Freccia D'Oro (4) of Gian Maria Cornaggia Medici and Mantegazza who with a final charge managed to get the better of the less powerful Lancia Aprilias of Perobelli and Cremonesi and "Ippocampo" and Mori, the latter pair having led the class from the Leghorn check-point to the one at Bologna.

4

The new Gran Turismo class was won by the Alfa Romeo 2500 SS Touring (1) of the Argentine driver Adolfo Schwelm and De Simone.

The Faina-bodied Patriarca Giannini (2), driven by the specialist and multiple Italian champion Sesto Leonardi together with Prosperi, won the 750 cc Sport class at a high average speed of over 105 kph, good enough for 24th place overall. Luigi Fagioli, paired with Diotallevi finally took the OSCA Mt4 (3) to a class win and finished seventh overall.

The Autocar, May, 4 1951

Ferraris triumph in Mille Miglia
Great Drive By Wisdom Wins Unlimited Closed Class For Aston Martin

Villoresi continued his run of successes since recovering from last year's serious accident by winning the Mille Miglia for the first time Sunday last. Although the course was shorter than last year's the weather was bad and the new section from Rome to Siena slow, winding and difficult, so Luigi, driving the 4,080 c.c. Ferrari coupé, did not equal the average speed of Giannino Marzotto with the 2,300 c.c. Ferrari on the longer route of last year. His speed of 75.70 m.p.h. was still a wonderful achievement. He slid off the road twice, damaging the front of the car, and summed up the difficulty of controlling a car with 240 b.h.p. and weighing under a ton on narrow roads through thick crowds and traffic by sayng: "I hope it doesn't rain, but for us it's raining all the time". A brilliant success by Bracco, driving the new 2-litre Lancia Aurelia Gran Turismo coupé, made him second in the race at 73.7 m.p.h. Third was Scotti (an amateur) on a 2,600 c.c. Ferrari, driving with Ruspaggiari, an ex-Alfa test driver. Fourth was Paolo Marzotto, who succeeded on the 2-litre Ferrari when his more famous brothers had retired on faster cars, and fifth Ippocampo, in another Aurelia.

Brescia was en fete as usual when the first small car in the production class – a baby Fiat – left at 9 p.m. on Saturday and the rest followed at minute intervals. But competitors soon met fierce storms, cutting visibility and turning roads into skating rinks. By the early hours of Sunday, when the fast sports cars were coming to the starting line, torrential rain struck Brescia, mercilessly lashing the crews of open cars, but did not discourage the crowds who crammed stands and lined the roadside under the glare of cinema floodlights and stabbing flashbulbs. They stayed until dawn, then adjourned for warming drinks at all-night cafés and bars before going on to church for early Mass. Although it did not reach last year's record, the total of 322 starters testified to the continual fascination of this mad race round Italy, and the event was more international than usual, with strong contingents from Britain and France plus others, including Greek, German and Argentine drivers.

Crashes in the downpour during the first two hours eliminated most of the British hopes, but Cortese brought a Frazer Nash into eight place, although the car had not been fully overhauled since its Sicily victory and finished with a broken pushrod. Wisdom, with Hume as passenger, made a fine run at 68.7 m.p.h. in the Aston Martin DB2 saloon to finish eleventh and win the unlimited class for closed or convertible cars. Among other useful items this earns £135 and a Vespa scooter.

Another old hand, Donald Healey, with son Geoffrey in the new Nash-Healey convertible, finished fourth in this class. Stapleton, with his wife as passenger, brought a stark pre-war 2,000 c.c. Aston Martin to ninth place in the sports 2-litre class against mass Ferrari opposition – a notable feat of endurance, for Italians regard finishing in the Mille Miglia as equal to a win in many other events.

The new class for production cars, with makers' bodywork and at least 250 made, was a great success, and attracted 149 starters, but unfortunately no British entries. The French con-

centrated their forces here in the 750 c.c. group with a flock of Dyna Panhards and Renaults. The Dyna Panhards took first, second and fourth places against dozens of Fiats, their larger engines and greater power fully compensating for lack of local knowledge on the part of the drivers. First place in this class went to rally drivers Descollanges and Grignoux, who had never seen the course before. One Dyna bonnet flew open at speed, butr the crew kept on the road and continued after lashing it down.

In the 1,100 c.c. production group, Fiat 1,100 c.c. cars took the first seven places while Lancias dominated the 1,500 c.c. category with Aprilias coming in the first nine places.

In the group for fast closed cars or convertibles, with bodies to international sports dimensions and at least 30 chassis of the type complete, the 750 c.c. class had special Fiats in the first four places. Cisitalias were first and second in the 1,100 c.c. group, followed by eight Fiats, while in the 2,000 c.c. group Lancia Aurelias held all the first ten places. The 750 and 1,100 c.c. sports categories produced the usual assortment of fast but sketchy Fiat specials, with minimum body-work, cycle wings and engines modified by such specialists as Stanguellini, Giannini, Ermini and Turolla, but the 1,100 c.c.results were dominated by the Maserati brothers' Osca cars in the first three places, the winner, Fagioli, being seventh

in the whole race, only three minutes behind Bonetto with the big 4,500 c.c. V-twelve Alfa, which now has new open bodywork. In the 2,000 c.c. category Cortese (Frazer Nash) was confronted by twelve Ferraris. Schwelm started fast in this group with a C6 Maserati, but retired with a broken half-shaft. As last year, treacherous conditions took a heavy toll in the first 150 miles, especially among the fast cars. Even among the little production cars the determination to average over 50 m.p.h. produced skids and collisions with walls and milestones; cars were in the ditch, cars were on fire. Ravasini overturned his Fiat, which, like Guenzani's Aurelia, burned out without damage to the crew.

Only 16 miles from the start Ascari, in an open 4,080 c.c. Ferrari, skidded into some parked cars at a bend and bounced into to crowd, two of whom were seriously hurt. Within a few minutes Johnson and Stirling Moss, in Jaguars, and Santori (Alfa) all piled up at the same spot. The crews were unhurt, but the cars were out. Johnson had split his fuel tank; Moss continued, but a damaged transmission forced his early retirement. Both had found their brakes inoperative when approaching the corner and were convinced that there was oil on the·road, but Ferraris blamed mud.

Soon afterwards Gatti, a Covent Garden fruit importer with an XK Jaguar, crashed into a road marking post and retired unhurt.

The Maserati A6GCS of Porrino-Savio (No. 349) finished 29th overall and is seen here alongside the Abarth 205 of the Lothaller-Anzenbacher pairing (did not start) and in front of the yellow Ferrari 166 MM of Palmer Aprile and Zaccaria Ferravazzi (No. 344).
Stirling Moss and "Rainbow" at the start with the works Jaguar (bottom).

Then Sydney Allard, with the Cadillac-engined car, who had done 77 miles in the first hour and 44 in the next half, passed a Ferrari and entered a bend at high speed, skidded into a mile-post, bent his axle and finished unhurt in a field. Meanwhile Biondetti was forcing the pace with his Jaguar Special, consisting of an XK engine, transmission and suspension, in a light Italian tubular chassis. But on a rough level crossing the chassis flexed, allowing the fan to cut the radiator hose and his hopes vanished.

Pressing On

By the Ravenna control, 190 miles from the start, it was clear that last year's winner, Giannino Marzotto, was now setting the pace. Driving a striking 2,600 c.c. Ferrari coupé with pillarless wind-screen, he coud probably take more liberties than Villoresi, who was embarrassed by excess power, and was leading him by five minutes at 84 m.p.h. average, with Serafini third on a

2,600 c.c. Ferrari. In the 2,000 c.c. sports class Schwelm (Maserati) was leading Paolo Marzotto at 78 m.p.h. average, while in the 1,100 c.c. sports class Oscas held the first five places. Bracco was already well in the lead in the 2,000 c.c.

closed cars class at over 80 m.p.h. average on his Aurelia coupé. Sighinolfi had maintained a terrific average, over 86 m.p.h., to Verona on a 1,100 c.c. Stanguellini, but he dropped out. At Sinigallia, Giannino Marzotto stopped with a broken rear axle;

then brother Vittorio retired at Fano with the third of the 4,1-litre Ferraris. This let Serafini into second place with a 2,600 c.c. Ferrari, four minutes behind Villoresi, but shortly before Pescara Serafini's Ferrari mounted a bank and crashed through some trees

GENERAL CLASSIFICATION

1. Ferrari 4,080 (Villoresi; Cassani), 12h 50 m 18s, 75.70 m.p.h.
2. Lancia Aurelia 1,990 (Bracco; Maglioli), 13h 10m 14s, 73.7 m.p.h.
3. Ferrari 2,600 (Scotti; Ruspagiari), 13h 22m 4s
4. Ferrari 2,000 (P. Marzotto; G. Marini), 13h 30m 48s
5. Lancia Aurelia 1,990 (Ippocampo: Mori), 13h 47m 30s
6. Alfa Romeo 4,500 (Bonetto: Casnaghi), 13h 49m 35s
7. Osca 1,100 (Fagioli; Borghi), 13h 52m 35s
8. Prazer-Nash 1,971 (Cortese: Togni), 14h 6m 28s
9. Osca 1,100 (Bordoni; Serbelloni), 14h 6m 49s
10. Osca 1,100 (Cabianca; Zanelli), 14h 7m 42s

CLASS RESULTS

Production Cars: 756 c.c.

1. Dyna Panhard (Descollanges; Gignoux), 17h 27m 17s, 55,67 m.p.h.
2. Dyna Panhard (Bianchi; Avetta), 17h 35m 7s
3. Fiat (Mazzi; Dallora), 17h 43m 29s

1,100 c.c.

1. Fiat 1,100 (Andreini; Quercioli), 16h 3m 49s 60.55 m.p.h.
2. Fiat 1,100 (Bobocca; Cavallo), 16h 20m 18s
3. Fiat 1,100 (Bevilacqua; Nascetti), 16h 22m 2s

1,500 c.c.

1. Lancia Aprilia (Anselmi; Gianni), 14h 42m 45s, 66.06 m.p.h.
2. Lancia Aprilia (Croce; Castello), 14h 55m 56s
3. Lancia Aprilia (Sculati; Massai), 15h 7m 1s

Closed or convertible cars: 750 c.c.

1. Fiat Zagato (Ferraguti; Faido), 16h 31m 32s, 58.81 m.p.h.
2. Fiat (Lunghi; Petreni), 17h 8m 59s
3. Fiat Zagato (Brambilla; Fusetti), 17h 50m 13s

1,190 c.c.

1. Cisitalia (Musitelli; Musitelli), 14h 34m 34s, 65.18 m.p.h.
2. Cisitalia (Bruni; Siena), 15h 17m 47s
3. Fiat (Braida; Borio), 15h 24m 17s

2,000 c.c.

1. Lancia Aurelia (Bracco)
2. Lancia Aurelia (Ippocampo)
3. Lancia Aurelia (Valenzano; Maggio), 13h 50m 0s

Over 2,000 c.c.

1. Aston Martin (Wisdom; Hume), 14h 7m 41s, 68.79 m.p.h.
2. Ferrari (Ammendola; Pinzero), 14h 13m 42s
3. Ferrari (Cornacchia; Mariani), 14h 17m 27s
4. Healey (D. Healey; G. Healey), 15h 5m 3s

Sports Cars: 750 c.c.

1. Fiat Giannini (Zannini; Bertozzo) 15h 25m 28s, 63.01 m.p.h.
2. Fiat (Stanga; Stanga), 15h 36m 3s
3. Fiat (Brandoli; Mazzonis), 15h 47m 54s

1,100 c.c.

1. Osca (Fagioli) 69.98 m.p.h.
2. Osca (Bordoni)
3. Osca (Cabianca)

2,000 c.c.

1. Ferrari (P. Marzotto), 71.92 m.p.h.
2. Frazer Nash (Cortese);
3. Ferrari (Masseroni; Vignolo), 14h 34 m 5s

Over 2,000 c.c.

1. Ferrari (Villoresi)
2. Ferrari (Scotti)
3. Alfa-Romeo (Bonetto; Casnaghi), 13h 49m 35s.

to drop into a field. The car was wrecked and the driver broke an arm and a leg. Schwelm retired soon afterwards; letting Paolo Marzotto's Ferrari into the lead in the 2,000 c.c. sports class, with Cortese already second. At Rome, 564 miles from the start, Villoresi was leading at just under 80 m.p.h., after seven hours 18 minutes of fast motoring; next came the astonishing Bracco, and third in the general classifica-

tion was the experimental Alfa of Borniglia – a short-chassis coupé like Rol's. Fourth place was held by Bordoni in a 1,100 c.c. Osca. Drivers found the new inland section, Rome-Bolsena-Radico-fani-Siena, extremely tiring; there were intermittent rain and fairly heavy traffic, fortunately most of the latter going in the same direc-tion as the race. After Florence came the dangerous Raticosa and Futa Passes, where there

are precipices with no retaining walls. Bornigia slid over the edge on the Fura at the point where two small cars had already gone over. His car fell sixty feet and landed on its wheels, but the dri-ver fractured his pelvis. Scotti and Ruspaggiari (Ferrari) were then third.

The weather was clearing as the fast cars tore past earlier starting small ones and swerved their way through Sunday-afternoon

traffic via Bologna, Modena, Pia-cenza and Cremona to Brescia, where thousands lined the streets in brilliant sunshine at last to watch the finish. Cars were mud-spattered and often bat-tered, but the crews of closed cars were often immaculate in lounge suits. Villoresi was quite unruffled on arrival, while Wisdom and Healey completed the day's motoring as they started – in tril-by hats.

Motor Sport, June, 1951

THE XVIII MILLE MIGLIA (APRIL 29th)

After Ascari and Serafini had both crashed, Villoresi brought another of the new 220-b.h.p., Type 346, "Inter-America" 4.1-litre sports-coupé Ferraris home first in this stupendous 970-mile race, last survivor of the great town-to-town races that virtually died with Paris-Madrid in 1903. Villoresi averaged over 75 1/2 m.p.h. in spite of a bad crash. Next home was Bracco, in a Lancia Aurelia saloon of only 2 llitres, a feat that is epic and ranks the latest Lancia as one of the world great cars. Scotti's 2.6-litre Ferrari was third, Marzotto's 2-litre fourth.

Cortese again drove well- remember the Tour de Sicily?- to finish eighth (second in his class), but even more outstanding was Fagioli's seventh place in a 1,100-c.c. Osca, at all but 70 m.p.h.

The intervening places went to another Lancia Aurelia and a 4 1/2-litre Alfa-Romeo.

Wisdom and Hume drove splendidly in a D.B.II Aston-Martin saloon to win the 3-litre class. The XK120 Jaguar engine of Biondetti's tubular-chassis special lost water due to a hose-leak and Moss and Johnson eliminated themselves when their XK120s skidded near the start. Allard also crashed. Stapleton and his wife put up a stout show by finishing, in an old Aston-Martin. So the 1951 Mille Miglia has come and gone and the battle transfers to Le Mans.

Top, the mayor of Brescia Bruno Boni congratulating Enzo Ferrari during the prize-giving gala held in the foyer of the Teatro Grande following the 18th edition of the Mille Miglia. In the foreground is the impressive Franco Mazzotti trophy awarded to Ferrari as the winning constructor.

Above, the over 2,000 c.c. class was won by T. Wisdom and A. Hume on Aston Martin.

1

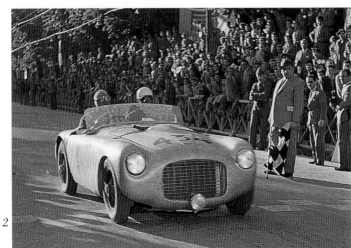

2

3

Overall victory went to the Ferrari 340 Vignale America berlinetta of Gigi Villoresi and Piero Cassani (4) at an average speed of 121.821 kph. The cars which caused the greatest surprise were, however, the semi-works Lancia Aurelia B20s of Giovanni Bracco-Umberto Maglioli (1) and "Ippocampo"-Mori (5) that finished second and fifth overall respectively. They also occupied the first two places overall in the Group "A" category reserved for fast closed and convertible cars, and the 2000 cc "A" class.

Splitting the two Turin cars was the Ferrari 212 S Motto (2) of Piero Scotti and Amos Ruspaggiari and the Ferrari 166 MM (3) of Paolo Marzotto who, together with Marino Marini, finished fourth overall and won the up to 2000 cc Sport class.

5

1

2

4

Among the cars entered in the international "B" category reserved for utility cars, victory in the 750 cc class went to the Panhard of Descollanges and Gignoux (1) with the similar car of Bianchi and Avetta second. The Fiat 500 Cs were penalised by their smaller engines. In the 1100 cc class the struggle amongst the Fiat 1100s saw Andreini and Quercioli (2) emerge victorious, whilst the 1500 cc class and category "B" overall was won by Anselmi and Gianni in a Lancia Aprilia (3). They finished 24th overall at an average speed of 106.304 kph. In category "B" victory in the 750 cc class went to the 750 MM of Sergio Ferraguti and Faido (4) at an average speed of 94.640 kph. The Musitelli brothers' old Cisitalia 202 (5) con the 1500 cc class whilst the over two-litre prize went to the glorious Aston Martin DB2 (6) of Tom Wisdom and Hume who beat the Ferrari of Amedola and Cornacchia with an average speed of 110.701 kph.

3

5

6

1

The 750 Sport class was won by the Pasqualin Giannini of Luigi Zanni- ni and Bertozzo (1), whilst Luigi Fagioli, this time paired with Borghi, repeated his success of the previous year with his OSCA Mt4 (2) and finished eighth overall.

2

MILLE MIGLIA

Bracco Drives Villoresi's 4.1-Litre Ferrari to Outright Victory at 79.9 m.p.h. Leslie Johnson Takes Seventh Place in General Classification in Nash Healey. Wisdom Has Class Win in Aston Martin. Moss Retires. Mercedes and Lancia Impressive

Brescia, Sunday Night.

The two leading protagonists of the 1952 Mille Miglia, the 19th in the series, were the Ferrari and Mercedes-Benz teams. The three cars used in this event by the Germans created great interest, being the new Type 330SL, based on the well-known Type 300. Protests were feared on the eve of the race about the type of vertical swinging doors used on these cars, but they appeared to obey the letter regulations. The Mercedes proved to be a strong challenger of the Ferrari, in fact, the one driven by Kling was in the lead for many miles, although at one time Taruffi seemed to be a possible winner, particularly when he suceeded in reducing the lead held by Kling. Ferrari used many variants in this year's race. The one driven by Taruffi was said to have a maximum power of no less than 300 h.p. from some 4-litres. There were many Ferraris with engines over 2,700 c.c. including that used by the winner, Giovanni Bracco. There were also 2-litre versions used by Bordoni and Brivio, the President of the Italian Sporting Commission. These cars were credited with a maxi-

mum of 145 h.p. In the Gran Turismo class there were many interesting cars, including new versions of the Aurelia, Alfa Romeo, Fiat V8 and Siata 208, which was also using a Fiat V8 engine and was competing in the sports category. This year's Alfa Romeo used two double Weber carburetters and a new rear suspension system. All

these cars are credited with a maximum speed of more than 130 m.p.h., but the drivers were not always able to use such speed because of the bad weather conditions which made the roads like an ice rink from Rome to the finish. Ferrari lost a high percentage of its force and owes its victory to Giovanni Bracco, who was called at the

last minute to take the place of Villoresi. At Verona, Bracco had averaged a speed of over 93 m.p.h. and at Ravenna he had gained five minutes from Kling. Taruffi started very carefully, partly because weather conditions prevented him from employing the full power of his car. In any case, it was expected that he would make his maximum effort after his home town Rome and after Florence over the Suta Pass. The Mille Miglia proverb says: "He who leads at Rome will never win at Brescia". Once again the truth of this has been proved. After Ravenna the tremendous speed of Bracco was reduced by tyre trouble. At L'Aquila he had lost 13 minutes to Kling, the latter having proved his skill and good judgment. Lang, pre-war ace of Mercedes, slid off the road and Caracciola had plug trouble. It was after Siena that the fight between Ferrari and Mercedes assumed a new aspect. Taruffi retired through mechanical trouble, but Bracco had reduced his disadvantage by 8 minutes and he won the duel over the Suta Pass. At Florence, Bracco had an advantage of 1 min. 30 secs., and at Brescia he won by 4 mins. 32 secs. While opinions differ about the correct method of training for the

Mille Miglia, it is interesting to note that such drivers as Tommy Wisdom, who won the over 2-litres Gran Turismo category, and Leslie Johnson, who was, as in 1950, the highest placed British car, both increased their efforts as the race progressed. Stirling Moss was eliminated at Bologna with a split fuel tank with a possible fourth place within his grasp. Donald Healey was forced out thorugh tyre trouble, and the third official Aston Martin, driven by George Abecassis, retired with clutch trouble. Wisdom had a trouble-free run with his Aston Martin, but Johnson's Nash Healey had shock absorber trouble for most of the race. Mercedes-Benz were in Italy for two months preparing for the race, and all cars and drivers did 16 practice tours, which must have cost at least £1,200 in petrol alone.

Donald Healey and his son Geoffrey with their Nash Healey berlinetta.Reg Parnell and Serboli (Aston Martin DB2) finished 13th overall. On the facing page, the Biondetti-Jaguar built by the talented Tuscan driver from the remains of his works XK 120 and entrusted to Pezzoli and Cazzulani.

Motor Sport, June 1952

MILLE MIGLIA,
OR THE WRITING ON THE WALL

The Mille Miglia, one of the greatest road races on the calendar and the sole survivor of the old town-to-town, public road contests, was a truly Homeric struggle this year. Germany showed the «writing on the wall» by arriving with the new coupé 300SL Mercédès-Benz some two months beforehand, covering the 1,000 miles of roads at least ten times, at a cost in fuel alone, the Daily Press emphasised, of some £2,000. But not yet did this teutonic thoroughness pay 100 per cent dividends. Karl Kling set a fast pace and led nearly to the finish, after he had overtaken Bracco's experimental light 2.7-litre V12 Ferrari coupé which was delayed with tyre trouble. Kling was hard-pressed by the 2,715-c.c. open Ferraris of Marzotto and Castellotti, then by Taruffi's new 300 b.h.p. G.P.-engined 4 1/2-litre Ferrari sports two-seater which blew up its transmission in the effort.

Kling was averaging nearly 93 m.p.h. in the wet, but team-mate Lang had left the road and retired and Caracciola's Mercédès-Benz was held by Abecassis in a DB2 Aston-Martin

Results:

lst	Bracco and Rolfo (2,700-c.c. Ferrari) 128.6 k.p.h. 12 hr. 9 min. 45 sec.	
2nd	Kling and Klenk (3,000-c.c. Mercedes-Benz) 12 hr. 14 min. 17 sec.	
3rd	Fagioli and Borghi (1,991-c.c. Lancia Aurelia) 12 hr. 40 min. 5 sec.	
4th	Caracciola (Mercedes-Benz)	
5th	Anselmi (Lancia Aurelia)	
6th	Ippocampo (Lancia Aurelia)	
7th	Johnson (Nash-Healey)	
8th	Amendola (Lancia Aurelia)	
9th	Brivio (Ferrari)	
10th	Bordoni (Ferrari).	

750 c.c. Sports – Marchese (Dyna Panhard)
15 hr. 35 min. 17 sec.

1,100 c.c. Sports – Cabianca (Osca)
13 hr. 32 min. 50 sec.

2,000 c.c. Sports – Brivio (Ferrari)
13 hr. 14 min. 22 sec.

Over 2,000 c.c. Sports – Bracco (Ferrari)
12 hr. 9 min. 45 sec.

750 c.c. Grand Touring – Gignoux (Dyna Panhard)
15 hr. 20 min. 24 sec.

1,500 c.c. Grand Touring – Lurani (Porsche)
14 hr. 53 min. 3 sec.

2,000 c.c. Grand Touring – Fagioli (Lancia Aurelia)
12 hr. 40 min. 5 sec.

Over 2,000 c.c. Grand Touring – Wisdom (Aston-Martin DB 2)   13 hr. 29 min. 49 sec.

750 c.c. Production Sports – Redele (Renault)
15 hr. 46 min. 15 sec.

1,100 c.c. Production Sports – Metternich (Porsche)
15 hr. 53 min. 39 sec.

1,500 c.c. Production Sports – Mazzonis (Lancia Aprilia)   15 hr. 27 min. 10 sec.

1,100 c.c. National Touring. – Matrullo (Fiat)
16 hr. 18 min. 28 sec.

1,500 c.c. National Touring – Monaco (Fiat)
15 hr. 49 min. 6 sec.

Over 1,500 c.c. National Touring – Maglioli (Lancia Aurelia)   13 hr. 58 min. 35 sec.

Military Vehicles – Costa (Alfa Romeo Matta)
16 hr. 54 min. 3 sec.

1) *The Lancia team at scrutineering.*
2) *The leader board in Piazza della Vittoria that allowed the various phases of the race to be followed.*

until the British car's clutch gave out.

Bracco was driving superbly meanwhile and was in the lead again at Bologna. More tyre trouble delayed him, but he repassed Kling, to lead the German by 1 min. 40 sec. at Modena, home of Ferrari, and win by 4 min. 32 sec. All eyes now focus on Le Mans, where the thorough Mercédès-Benz team will again meet the weight of Ferrari opposition. In third place came the Lancia Aurelia of Fagioli, a stupendous effort by a veteran driver and in a car of the 2-litre Grand Touring class at that—

ahead of so many near-racers! It was a brilliant reflection of Bracco's great second place in an Aurelia last year and should do Lancia a power of good commercially. Moss drove the Type C Jaguar nearly into third place, but had to retire at the end with fuel tank leaks and steering trouble. Leslie Johnson was first Britisher home, a gallant seventh in a 4.1-litre prototype Nash-Healey. Tommy Wisdom in the 1951 DB2 won the big Grand Touring class for Aston-Martin, after Parnell had been delayed in his DB2 after hitting a milepost, and running out of fuel. Donald Healey had a narrow escape, his Healey bursting a tyre and wrecking itself on a bridge. In this fantastic race of 502 starters some retired and crashes took the lives of two Italian drivers in small Fiats, Grazzani and Avalle. Lancia Aurelias took fifth, six and eighth places, the 1900 Alfa-Romeos nothing higher than 17th place.

The Nash Healey of Johnson and McKenzie at the start. The British team finished in an excellent seventh place overall.

1

Giovanni Bracco and Alfonso Rolfo defended the Ferrari honour by winning the race at an average speed of 128.591 kph with their Ferrari 250 Vignale berlinetta (2), but this edition of the race was notable for the demonstration of efficiency provided by the Mercedes 300 SLs. Karl King (4), paired with Klenk, finished second, five minutes behind the winner, whilst the aged Rudolph Caracciola (3, and second in line in photo 2) finished fourth. The Aurelia B 20 Corsas of Luigi Fagioli (1) and Enrico Anselmi (5) came home 1st and 2nd in the Gran Turismo Internazionale class, and 3rd and 5th overall.

2

3

4

5

The Alfa Romeo AR 51 "Matta" driven by Captain Costa and Lieutenant Verga won the special class reserved for military vehicles (1), whilst the Fiat 500 C (6) of Lunghi and Landi won the 750 cc Turismo Nazionale class at an average speed of 88.089 kph, following the disqualification of Recordati-Bigi (2) for technical irregularities. In the 1100 cc class victory went to Matrullo and Conti with the Fiat (3), whilst among the 1500s, Ottorino Monaco and Sergio Ferraguti got the better of their rivals with the De Sanctis-tuned Fiat 1400 (5), reaching Brescia at an average speed of 98.872 kph.

While the first three classes of the Turismo Nazionale category were one-make affairs, in the over 1500 cc class, the powerful teams entered by Alfa Romeo and Lancia met head-to-head. The eventual winner at an average speed of over 111 kph was the Lancia B 21 (4) of Umberto Maglioli and Monteferrario, 19th overall, from the Alfa 1900 of Bruno Ruffo and Artesiani.

1

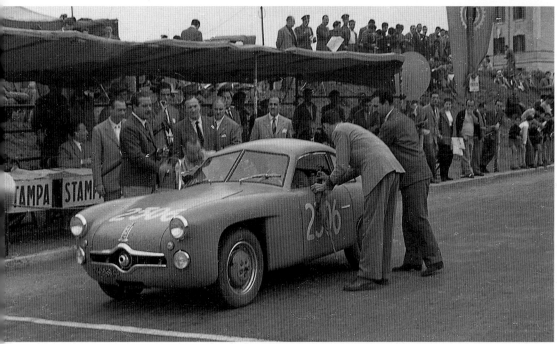

2

In the 750 cc class of the production sports car category the French pair of Redelé and Pons won with their Renault 4 CV 1063 (3). In the 1100 cc class, victory went to the Porsche (4) of Von Metternich and Einsiedel at an average speed of over 98 kph. Vittorio Mazzonis and Marsaglia won their class and the category overall with the Aprilia at 101.211 kph (7). Among the GTIs, following the exclusion of the DB of Gignoux and Touzot (2), victory in the 750 cc class went to the Zagato 750 MM (1) of Zafferi and Crivelli.

3

4

The 1500 cc class was won by the Porsche 356 (5) of Lurani and Berckleim while the over 2-litre class was taken for the second year running by the Aston Martin DB 2 (6) of Wisdom and Lown.

5

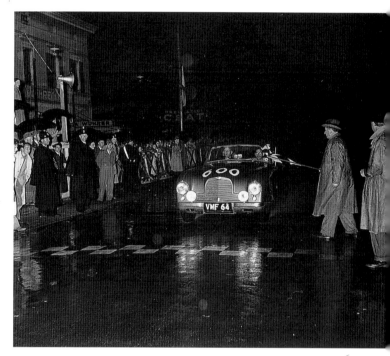

6

7

The excellent performance of the French cars in the minor categories was confirmed by the victory of Giacinto Marchese and Palvarini in the 750 SI class with the Panhard Allemano (1) prepared for Gastone Crepaldi's Italfrance team by Tino Bianchi. Giulio Cabianca and Gianfranco Roghi confirmed the supremacy of the OSCA in the 1100 cc class (2).

Antonio Brivio, president of the CSAI, and Piero Cassani avoided the embarrassing confrontation with the Lancia Aurelia by entering the Ferrari 166 MM Vignale (3) in the 2000 cc Sport class, thus earning a class win while finishing half an hour down on the Aurelia of Luigi Fagioli. Luciano Gianni and Raboni won (according to certain sources) the Index of Performance with the Fiat 500 C fitted with a Superba cylinder head (4). On the facing page, the Aston Martin of Parnell and Klementaski at the start.

A MERCILESS MILLE MIGLIA

Grand Prix Speeds Cause Mechanical - Slaughter in Event Won by Marzotto (Ferrari). Parnell (Aston Martin) Fifth

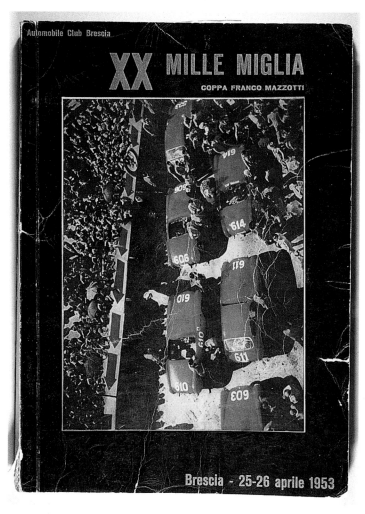

No motor race of modern times, not even the fabulous Targa Florio, breathes quite the romance of the Mille Miglia, last of the classics in the pioneer tradition of racing over open roads from city to city with an entry list of hundreds of cars ranging from the fastest sports cars in the world, driven by the great champions, to home-tuned runabouts driven by enthusiastic private owners - for to drive in the Mille Miglia is every young Italian driver's great ambition.

The very recital of the names of the cities through which the race runs its 938-mile course sounds like a race round the Renaissance. The start and finish is in the Lombard city of Brescia, sheltered by the wall of the Alps. Then the route runs east through Verona, past Juliet's balcony. Vicenza of the Paladian palaces, Padua, the university city, and then turns south through Ferrara, famous for sword blades and armour. Rimini, on the Adriatic coast, and, with a detour inland, back to the coast at Ravenna, with Dante's tomb. Now comes a fast coast road down to Pesaro, Fano and Ancona, and on again along the Adriatic through the Abruzzi to Pescara. Here the route turns west through the mountains to Popoli and l'Aquila, through the square with a fountain of 99 jets and out on the road to Rome, where the control is placed in the outskirts. The return route strikes north to Viterbo in Latium, encircled in battlements, Siena in Tus-cany, city of artists, and so to Lorenzo the Magnificent's Florence. The next stage has proved decisive in this remarkable race, for across the Arno the road coils over the Futa and Raticosa passes through the Apennines to the control at Bologna, once a powerful republic. Striking north-west, the route passes Modena of the Ghirlandia tower - and the Ferrari factory - Reggio. Parma with Correggio's painted dome, Piacenza of the Farnese family, and turns north again to Cremona of the violin makers and so back onto the Lombardy plain to Brescia, completing the gigantic figure-of-eight. Throughout the route, every village street is packed, every city square a sea of faces which only opens at the last moment to let the cars shoot through at 100 m.p.h. over the tram lines. Police and troops line the course, as excited as the spectators, and if any local insists on his right to drive on the officially open road, his life is in some danger from the populace as well as from the cars as they come sliding and braking through the tortuous Italian streets. Even in the open country the crowds come in from the entire region to line the roads, shouting themselves hoarse as the drivers flash past - the man at the wheel cool and confident, the co-driver crouching in what looks so like terror.

The Ferrari 340 MM Touring of Gi-gi Villoresi struggles through the crowd of enthusiasts to reach the scrutineering paddock. Villoresi's race ended with a broken differential near Ravenna.

Sunday, April 26

FROM GRANDE VITESSE, BRESCIA

At least 3,000 citizens of Brescia packed the piazza during the final day of the scrutiny of the cars, all talking at the tops of their voices while loudspeakers blared music and three aeroplanes wheeled and dived low overhead.

The Aston Martins and the Jaguars had been checked in the comparative calm of the preceding days but when the Alfa Romeos and Ferraris arrived at noon on the Saturday the multitude broke the cordons and the cars were lost for a time under a human tide.

The legendary Disco Volante body which is rumoured to have a tendency to lift at high speeds was not used, and the four works Alfa Romeos had the 3-litre chassis with De Dion rear and hastily built saloon bodies instead.

The works Ferraris were all open cars of the familiar type, three with 3-litre engines and Farina's with the 4 1/2-litre Formula I Grand Prix type of engine.

In this race, where the biggest class is merely labelled "over 2-litres" it is extremely difficult to discover quite what engines are under any of the car's bonnets.

LANCIA NOVELTIES

The new 3-litre Lancias proved to be V-8s with twin overhead camshafts to each bank and the unusual arrangement of inboard brake drums in front as well as in rear, the front drums driven by short shafts from the wheels. Lurani's Le Mans V-8 Fiat saloon (1,500 c.c.) had five speeds and was to be driven by Cortese. Most of the fast Italian cars had the Pirelli Mille Miglia tyre with a squiggly tread first used last year. The new 1,100 c.c. Fiat with its rather square English-looking saloon body was said to reach 80 m.p.h. with ease. Johnson's Jaguar XK120C and all the Healeys had overdrive to solve the problem of correct ratios for the long

straights on the Adriatic coast and the winding mountain passes. Farina, new to the race after so many years of absence, had taken the thing very seriously and had done at least six practice laps. The Jaguars and Astons, of course, had been practising steadily for a couple of weeks. Bracco, 1952 winner who found time to smoke 100 cigarettes while winning the race, had the latest 3-litre Ferrari V-12 with three quadruple carburetters. One of the more amusing incidents was the invasion of the Hotel Vittoria by the crowd who pressed noses against windows watching Pomeroy at tea in magnificent isolation under the impression he was Roberto Rossellini, who

was to drive a Ferrari. The Prince Aly Khan's Alfa Romeo was confided to pre-war driver Goffredo Zehender. Wharton's Cooper not being ready he was a non-starter.

NIGHT CLIMAX

The day passed in a whirl of emotion in the crowded streets and squares of the old city. Racing cars tore up and down in the traffic as if the race had already begun. As night fell, the long avenue where the start takes place leaped into light, dense crowds lined the roadside when at 9 p.m. last Saturday, under a clear moonlit Italian sky, with a warm night and no wind the 750 c.c. touring cars howled off one after the other, followed without cessation all night by the rest of the gigantic entry of well over 600 cars, until the over 2-litre sports class, headed by John Fitch's white-and-blue Nash-Healey went off at minute intervals at 5.40 a.m. on Sunday, with Tony Rolt's Jaguar XK120C bringing up the rear, in the pale light of the erly dawn. As the light strengthened and the last cars shot down the launching ramp and away towards Verona, heavy clouds began to roll over the mountains and, 100 miles to the east, it had been raining on the little 750 c.c. tourers, al-

60

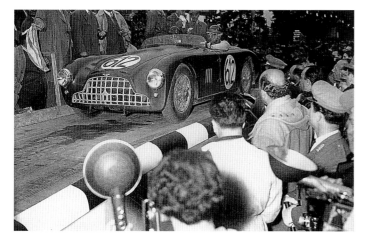

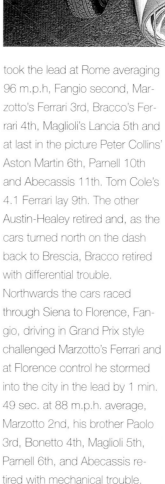

ready scuttling south to Pescara. On the dry roads out of Brescia speeds were higher than ever, and the fast men were belting through the villages, horns at full blast, at over 140 m.p.h.

First news was flashed from Verona, some 80 miles away: 1st Sanesi (Alfa Romeo); 2nd, Taruffi (3-litre Lancia) and 3rd, Farina (Alfa Romeo), with a race average of 111,8 m.p.h. The winner obviously lay in this rapid class where, of the 45 starters there were 16 Ferraris (saloons and open), 10 saloon Lancias, seven Jaguars, four Aston Martins (one saloon), three Alfa Romeo saloons, two Austin-Healeys open, with big windscreens, and one each of Lincoln (saloon), Nash-Healey, Gordini.

There was a shower of rain and sodden wet roads for the fast cars as they stormed on the long straights to Verona at record speed. Fate struck at the Jaguars - Johnson sent out with a split tank, Moss with back axle trouble, leaving Rolt out on his own. Likewise Fitch retired with brake trouble on the 4.1-litre Nash-Healey.

At Ravenna, 188 miles from the start, Sanesi led at 108.3 m.p.h. compared with Bracco's 88,7 m.p.h. last year in the rain, with Farina 1 min. 56 sec. behind,

then Kling, Bordoni on the 2.3-litre Gordini, Fangio and Bracco. Hawthorn at this control came up into 9th place behind Bonetto. Now Wisdom broke his back axle, Lockett retired on the Austin-Healey, Villoresi had engine trouble and Descollanges (Jaguar) had a terrible crash, driving clean off the road down a steep bank upside down, from which his co-driver was lifted, dead.

And now the battle became a slaughter in this sports-car race run at Grand Prix speed. After the 150 m.p.h. straights along the Adriatic coast Sanesi fled at a record average of 110,4 m.p.h. for the 300 miles, still well in the lead, chased by Farina and Giannino Marzotto on the Ferraris, Fangio and Kling on the other two Alfa Romeo saloons and Bonetto (Lancia). There had been several crashes among the smaller cars and Metternich's Porsche hit a spectator. Taruffi went out with engine trouble. The holocaust now began. Hawthorn went out followed by Bordoni's 2.3 Gordini; Rolt's Jaguar was in trouble, fell back, and was engulfed by the traffic of the reopened roads. Then through the mountain roads between Pescara and Rome Sanesi finally blew up followed almost at once by Farina so that Kling

took the lead at Rome averaging 96 m.p.h., Fangio second, Marzotto's Ferrari 3rd, Bracco's Ferrari 4th, Maglioli's Lancia 5th and at last in the picture Peter Collins' Aston Martin 6th, Parnell 10th and Abecassis 11th. Tom Cole's 4.1 Ferrari lay 9th. The other Austin-Healey retired and, as the cars turned north on the dash back to Brescia, Bracco retired with differential trouble. Northwards the cars raced through Siena to Florence, Fangio, driving in Grand Prix style challenged Marzotto's Ferrari and at Florence control he stormed into the city in the lead by 1 min. 49 sec. at 88 m.p.h. average, Marzotto 2nd, his brother Paolo 3rd, Bonetto 4th, Maglioli 5th, Parnell 6th, and Abecassis retired with mechanical trouble. Now up and over the Futa and

Raticosa where the road spans the Apennines on its way to Bologna the Fangio-Marzotto duel went on and this time Marzotto led into the city at 85,2 m.p.h. by a clear 2 min.57 sec. in front of Fangio, Paolo Marzotto 3rd, Bonetto 4th and Tom Cole in fifth place.

Sterzi passed Parnell into 6th place and Biondetti's Lancia was on Parnell's tail.

As the afternoon wore on the cars streamed back through Cremona on to the Lombardy Plain and even the closing stages were not devoid of drama.

Paolo Marzotto's Ferrari burst into flames within the last 20 miles and a little Fiat scuttling home in the small car class took the last corner of the race too fast and rolled over.

Motor Sport, June 1953

FERRARI – ALFA-ROMEO DUEL AT RECORD SPEED

Giannino Marzotto, winner of the XXth Mille Miglia at 142.347 k.p.h. with a 4.1 litre Ferrari

Bologna, April 26th.

FROM OUR CONTINENTAL CORRESPONDENT.

I have just seen all hell let loose upon the roads of Italy for 21 solid hours and my mind is a chaos of open exhausts, screaming tyres, hot sun and shouting Italians; but let us go back to the beginning. The Editor thought it would be a good idea if we looked at the XXth Mille Miglia on April 25/26th through the eyes of the Italian public, instead of from the seclusion of the Press bureau at Brescia. The Mille Miglia is run on a time basis, cars starting at minute intervals, half-minutes for the small ones, and as they cover the 1,512 kilometres on one circuit it is not possible to sit in one place and watch the racing, so the normal thing to do when trying to keep track of over 400 cars circulating Italy is to follow the racing by figures. That is to say, you station yourself at the start-and-finish, at Brescia, and compute the figures of times that come from the various controls around the route, so that last year, for example, everyone was very excited about the closeness of Bracco and Kling, even though they never set eyes on either car.

My plan was to watch the competitors go past a point about

two hours distant from Brescia, there calculating the leaders, drive like mad over the mountains and meet them coming up the west coast, again calculating the positions and then get the final positions at Brescia when all the tumult and shouting had died down.

The atmosphere of the Mille Miglia spreads over the borders of Italy and going down through France I heard reports that the Healeys were on their way through Switzerland, that the Aston-Martins had been in Italy for some time; and as I neared the Italian Alps D.B. Panhards, rorty-sounding 4-cv Renaults, an Alfa and a Porsche all went by already wearing their racing numbers, which for those starting from 22.00 hours Saturday night and onwards, was the actual starting time in hours and minutes. Along the Autostrada from Turin to Brescia the pace quickened and Lancia Aurelia Gran Turismos, Alfa-Romeo Sprints, more Porsches, a works 2-litre Ferrari and a 4.1 Ferrari all hurried by. Brescia itself was boiling over with frenzy and had been for days, and the scrutineering and checking was being done in the Piazza Vittoria, long-since closed to normal traffic and now a seething mass of spectators, officials, competing cars and ice-

On the facing page, the start with the Austin Healey 100 of Lockett and Reid (above) and the Jaguar C-Type of Moss and Goodall. Right, the Aston Martin DB3 of Peter Collins and Ken, 16th overall at the Brescia finish.

cream sellers. Just before midday on Saturday the frenzy reached its limit when the official Ferraris arrived, led by the one and only Enzo himself in a new 1,100 Fiat. The crowd screamed, the officials shouted, the loudspeakers nearly burst and the Ferraris sounded wonderful. Sterzi had an open 2-litre, Paolo Marzotto and Bracco 3-litre coupés, Giannino Marzotto, Tom Cole, Farina and Cabianca had open 4.1-litres, and Hawthorn an open 3-litre. Villoresi's car was there but without him. The pandemonium had only just died down when a fresh outburst started at the entrance to the square as the new Alfa-Romeo coupés arrived.

The crowd was so thick and uncontrollable that it was some time before the cars could get to the scrutineers. Fangio, Kling and Sanesi had 3.6-litre six-cylinders, while Zehender had a 2-litre four-cylinder, but outwardly they were all the same size, which was exceedingly small, the tops of the roofs being well below shoulder-height. Although the commentator insisted on calling them Disco-Volantes, they were nothing like the open versions so far as the body was concerned, being typical Italian sports-racing coupés, or Berlinettas. Mechanically they

were the same as the much-vaunted Disco-Volantes, having double wishbone and coil-spring i.f.s. and de Dion rear, with inboard brakes of vast width and the de Dion tube positioned by a transverse Panhard rod. The cockpit was very small, with a centrally-operated five-speed gearbox and a system of air-venting to control the interior heat. In the sloping tail was a vast fuel tank and rearward visibility was virtually nil. The exhaust pipes were in three pairs running into an expansion-box and a sort of megaphone under the passenger's door. After lunch comparative peace descended on the town for a while and everyone prepared for the beginning

of this fantastic marathon, which was scheduled to start at 9 p.m. The works Maseratis were ready for action, sitting in their garages watched over by two mechanics, the Gordini in the over 2-litre class was being tried along part of the route by Bordoni, the driver, while various other competitors were working on their cars or rushing about the town, depending on whether they had a "near" racing-car or a standard saloon. Leaving Brescia, which was beginning to get on the boil again, I motored across country to a short distance from Ravenna, on the Adriatic coast, the first control point and some 265 kilometres from the start. Arriving at a very fast section of narrow

bumpy road I drew off and awaited the first arrival. All was peace and quiet, the moon was bright and the only sound was the croaking of the frogs until just on midnight—when it happened! The peace of the countryside was rudely broken and remained broken until nearly 9 a.m. Being on the first section of the course the cars came by more or less in class order, though of the 750-c.c. Touring Class the Panhards were already way ahead and going past absolutely flat-out, followed at intervals by Renaults and Fiats, all driven at peak revs., having come down a long, straight hill, under a railway bridge and round a 100 m.p.h. bend. It was not long before the humming of standard engines was interrupted by the first car in the 750-c.c Sports Class, as a Fiat-Stanguellini went by with a crackle from its twin-cam engine that could be heard for nearly half-a-minute after it had passed. This was the prelude to the faster entries and D.B. Panhards crackling on their twin-cylinders, Erminis, Morettis, Gianninis, Siatas and 1,083 Renaults all shattered the moonlit night. The 1,300-c.c. Touring Class, consisting mostly of the new 1,100 Fiats, followed and then the 2,000-c.c. Touring Class which was dominated by 1,900 Alfa-

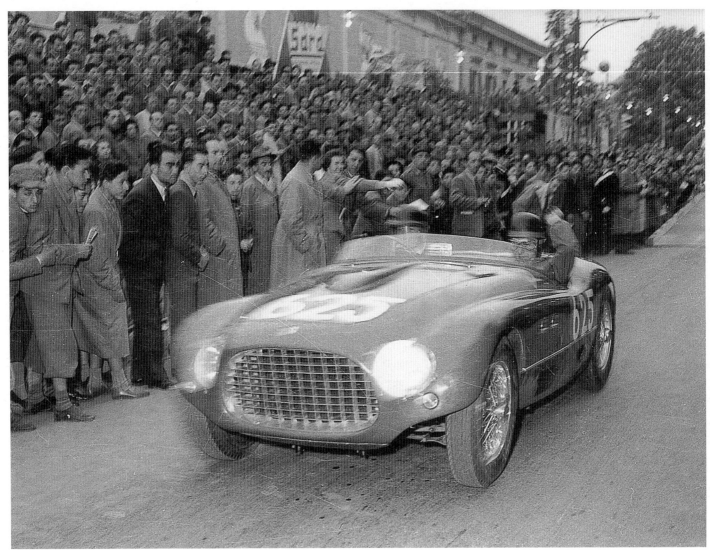

Romeos, with a good sprinkling of Lancia Aurelias intermingled. The 1,900s had obviously got the class well in hand and went by at a very impressive speed with remarkable stability considering the uneven road. As the last few Alfa-Romeos went by daylight arrived and with it the really fast categories. First the 1,100-c.c. Sports Class, and it was the open Osca driven by Sani that arrived first, followed very closely by that of Venezian. When Sgor came by in his Osca, it was seen that he was leading the class, and the clock was put on the 2,000-c.c. Sports Class. It was not long before they came through, Capelli on an 8V Fiat coupé and Sterzi on a 2-litre Ferrari being well ahead of sched-

ule, then Cortese on another Fiat coupé equalling their time, as did Casella with a works Gordini, painted red for the occasion. Just after 7 s.m. the air was rent by the sound of an engine turning at over 7,000 r.p.m. and the first of the works A6G Maseratis came down the hill and under the railway bridge and Musso went by, leading the class by nearly 3 minutes. Soon after came Mantovani and Giletti with the other two team cars, all of them sounding wonderful in the stillness of the morning. They were literally two-seater versions of the Formula II cars, complete with "spiky" brakes, and A-bracket-controlled, 1/4 – elliptically – sprung rear axle, and with left-hand drive, the whole chassis

covered by the bare minimum of all-enveloping body. A few minutes after Giletti had passed, Zehender went by with the 2-litre Alfa-Romeo coupé making second fastest time to my point. One minute later there was the most shattering spectacle as a blue and red open 4.1 Ferrari came into sight, cutting for the bend and then accelerating by at over 130 m.p.h. on a bumpy 30-ft. road, looking, completely out of control. It was Giannino Marzotto and almost at the same time his brother Paolo passed with the 3-litre coupé. Then things happened fast and furiously, for the over-2,000-c.c. Sports Class was upon me. Giannino passed me at 7.31 a.m. and having started at 5.47 it

meant he had taken 1 hour 44 minutes up to my point on the course. Peter Collins went by in a 2.9-litre Aston-Martin DB III, a heartening sight at that early hour, and then came Fangio with the first of the Alfas, closely followed by Kling. They were noticeably steadier than the Ferraris and just as quick, their times being 1 hour 46 minutes and 1 hour 45 minutes, respectively, then Bordoni passed in the works Gordini at 1 hour 45 minutes, also Bonetto with the first of the new works 2.9-litre Lancia coupés, bearing no similarity to previous cars from that factory. These new cars were built on "space-frames", had trailing-link-type i.f.s., inboard brakes all round, and were very light. His

On the facing page, the Ferrari 250 MM bodied by Vignale and driven by Hawthorn and Cappi. Right, the fourth works Aston Martin, the DB2 of Wisdom and Halliwell.

time was only two minutes slower than the Gordini and then the "fastest-yet" arrived, Farina in the open 4.1 Ferrari closely followed by Bracco with the coupé. Farina had not only made up seven minutes on Bracco at this stage, but was down to 1 hour 40 minutes and looked really immense as he passed at over 130 m.p.h., the car snaking about the road and looking a handful. There followed Cole, going much slower, Parnell and Abecassis with the other two DB IIIs, Carini and Biondetti with new Lancias and then at nine minutes past 8 a.m. Sanesi went by in the third of the works Alfa-Romeos, going noticeably faster than anything so far and as he had started at 6.31 a.m. it put him well in the lead, with 1 hour 38 minutes. By that standard Hawthorn's 1 hour 47 minutes seemed slow while Rolt with Wisdom's Type C Jaguar seemed pathetic. Wisdom himself was driving an Aston-Martin DB II coupé and was only five minutes down on the works DB IIIs, which was a first-class effort. By 9 a.m. the last of this high-speed procession had passed and there was time to take stock. Among those missing already were Villoresi and Taruffi and most of the English cars. The former had gone out with rear axle trouble, the new

Lancia had engine trouble and the English cars had also retired. Moss on the only real works Jaguar, had broken his back-axle, Johnson had a split fuel tank on his own white XK120C, and the Austin-Healeys of Lockett and Hadley were stopped with clutch trouble, while Fitch had also stopped with the Nash-Healey.

Leaving the course and driving over cart-tracks, up and down 1 in 4 gradients and along parts of good roads I got to Bologna as the first of the small cars went through. At my point on the outward journey the general order had been Sanesi, Farina, G. Marzotto, Kling, Bordoni, Fangio, Bracco, P. Marzotto, Hawthorn and Bonetto. By more driving along mountain ledges, down cart-tracks and down descents up which there was no hope of return I made my way to a village at the foot of the Futa pass just before the run-in to Bologna. Al-

though the roads are not officially closed for this race there is no hope of driving along the course, for every man in Italy with a gun and a uniform makes it his personal responsibility to see that no one gets in the way of the competitors. The main road out of Bologna was very much shut off with guards at every crossing, while in the village I was at, two people were "pinched" for riding moto-scooters along the grass verge. If you wanted to move you went on foot or wheeled your push-bike or motor-cycle and there was no leniency. As the competitors in the slower categories came through the reason could be appreciated for they were using every inch of the road and taking blind bends in the village on the very limit of tyre adhesion. At this point, more than three-quarters of the way round the course, the numbers were greatly depleted while many cars bore signs of a hard passage,

with torn bumpers, dented wings and dented door-panels. Particularly noticeable was the tattered state of the 1,900 Alfa-Romeo saloons in general. They were still going incredibly quickly but nearly everyone had made contact with some hard object on the southern part of the course. The 1,100-c.c. Sports Class was still dominated by the Oscas, Venezian now being in the lead with Sani close behind, while the previous leader, Sgor, did not come through. The day was now very dry and hot as only Italy can be and towards 3 p.m. the time drew near for the leaders in the faster categories to arrive. While we wen anticipating the 2-litre Class there was a shattering roar, a screaming of tyres, a strong smell of hot oil and Giannino Marzotto went through, using all the road fighting the 4.1 in a series of juggles with steering and throttle, his passenger looking very worn and

haggard. The time was six minutes past 3 p.m. which meant a total time of 9 hours 19 minutes and a higher speed than had ever been recorded before. Obviously the Ferrari-Alfa duel was forcing a terrific pace. It was reported that Sanesi had retired, Kling had led at the Rome control but retired after that, Farina was out and Fangio had been in the lead on the other side of the mountains at Florence. If Fangio was to retain his lead he had to come by at 3.21 p.m. and at 3.24 the fierce-looking Alfa-Romeo coupé with the yellow grille went by, closely followed by Paolo Marzotto, which meant that Giannino was now leading by three minutes, after nine and a half hours racing at an average of over 137 k.p.h. When Marzot-

to reached the Bologna control Ferrari himself was awaiting him and told him to give the 4.1 its head on the very fast stretch to Cremona and thence to Brescia. This meant cruising at speeds which tend to make the mind boggle, for the road is wide, straight and smooth as far as the eye can see and with nearly 300 b.h.p. available it is quite likely that the estimated 270 k.p.h. was approached. Bracco being out there was no other opposition for these two, Tom Cole was driving steadily and Cabianca was rather slow, probably finding the difference between a Ferrari and a 1,350-c.c. Osca quite difficult. Hawthorn had retired and the Lancias were not quick enough to cope with the giants. As the afternoon wore on tired

and battered motor cars went by, still being driven hard, still being cornered near the limit, all hoping to last out the final 240 kilometres to the finish. Parnell went by looking very dirty and weary, but still well on time, Collins had dropped back a long way and had a big dent in the tail, while Abecassis had retired. The only works-supported Jaguar to be seen on the outward run had passed out with engine trouble. In the 2-litre Class the Alfa-Romeo coupé had retired, Musso had crashed his A6G Maserati and Giletti went by with Mantovani close behind, both sounding superbly fresh, while Casella with the works Gordini was third. Eventually, at 6 p.m., the armed forces were allowed to rest and the roads of Italy took

on their normal role, becoming a seething mass of frustrated motorists and motorcyclists. On the final run to Brescia Giannino Marzotto had followed his instructions and given the Ferrari all it had got, with the result that he finished nearly twelve minutes in front of Fangio, at an average speed of 142.347 k.p.h.–a fantastic average for ten-and-a-half hours driving and a new record for the Mille Miglia. Some way back came Bonetto in third place with one of the new Lancias, a promising debut in the Mille Miglia, fourth was Tom Cole, having driven a wisely-careful race with a car that is about the most potent thing in present-day racing, all categories included, and fifth was Parnell with the Aston-Martin DB III, England's only hope in real racing, but a good one nevertheless. Equally valorous ware the various class winners, for while driving a 4.1 Ferrari to win outright is a magnificent achievement, to cover the same course in a standard saloon or a diminutive sports 750-c.c. car is no mean feat. In the Touring Classes for strictly standard machines the 750-c.c. Class was won by Angelelli and Recchi with a 4-cv Renault, the 1,300-c.c. Class by Mancini with a new 1,100 Fiat, numbers of which had shown wonderful

MILLE MIGLIA 1,512 Kms. Warm and Dry		
GENERAL CLASSIFICATION		
1st. G. Marzotto (Ferrari 4.1 litre)	10 hr. 37 min. 19 sec.	142.347 k.p.h.
(88.23 m.p.h.)		
2nd. J. M. Fangio (Alfa-Romeo 3.6 litre)	10 hr. 49 min. 03 sec.	139.773 k.p.h.
3rd. F. Bonetto (Lancia 2.9 litre)	11 hr. 07 min. 40 sec.	135.876 k.p.h.
4th. T. Cole (Ferrari 4.1 litre)	11 hr. 20 min. 39 sec.	
5th. R. Parnell (Aston-Martin 2.9 litre)	11 hr. 32 min. 43 sec.	
6th. E. Giletti (Maserati A6G 2 litre)	11 hr. 38 min. 42 sec.	
7th. E. Anselmi (Lancia Aurelia G.T.)	11 hr. 41 min. 07 sec.	
8th. C. Biondetti (Lancia 2.9 litre)	11 hr. 49 min. 49 sec.	
9th. G. Cabianca (Ferrari 4.1 litre)	11 hr. 51 min. 39 sec.	
10th S. Mantovani (Maserati A6G 2 litre)	11 hr. 51 min. 56 sec.	

New Record: Marzotto 142.347 k.p.h. Old Record: Biondetti in 1938 135.381 k.p.h.

750 c.c. Touring:

1st. Angelelli-Recchi (Renault).	15 hr. 46 min. 12 sec.	95.878 k.p.h.
2nd. Bianchedi-Tabanelli (Panhard).	15 hr. 50 min. 55 sec.	
3rd. Porfiri-Caratti (Panhard).	15 hr. 59 min. 08 sec.	

1,300 c.c. Touring:

1st. Mancini-Mancini (Fiat 1 100).	14 hr. 05 min. 16 sec.	107.327 k.p.h.
2nd. Serena-Piccolo (Fiat 1,100).	14 hr. 05 min. 31 sec.	
3rd. Chidoni-Testolini (Fiat 1,100).	14 hr. 10 min. 52 sec.	

2,000 c.c. Touring:

1st. Pagliai-Parducci (Alfa-Romeo 1,900).	12 hr. 34 min. 05 sec.	120.305 k.p.h.
2nd. Stagnoli-Guiseppe (Alfa-Romeo 1,900).	12 hr. 37 min. 33 sec.	
3rd. Bormioli-Marchiori (Alfa-Romeo 1.900).	12 hr. 40 min. 46 sec.	

Unlimited Touring:

1st. Frere-Milhoux (Chrysler)	13 hr. 38 min. 03 sec.	110.898 k.p.h.

No other finishers

750 c.c. Sports:

1st. Touzot-Persillon (D.B. Panhard).	14 hr. 15 min. 36 sec.	106.031 k.p.h
2nd. Castellarin-Capaccioli (D.B. Panhard)	14 hr. 15 min. 46 sec.	
14 hr. 42 min. 46 sec.		
3rd. Anna Peduzzi-Goldani (Fiat-Stanguellini).	14 hr. 48 min. 57 sec.	

1,100 c.c. Sports:

1st. Venezian-Albarelli (Osca).	12 hr. 04 min. 50 sec.	125.160 k.p.h.
2nd. Sani-Bianchi (Osca).	12 hr. 26 min. 35 sec.	
3rd. Bormioli-Ficai (Fiat).	14 hr. 04 min. 34 sec.	

2,000 c.c. Sports:

1st. Giletti-Bertocchi (Maserati A6G).	11 hr. 38 min. 42 sec.	129.841 k.p.h
2nd. Mantovani-Palazzi (Maserati A6G).	11 hr. 51 min. 56 sec.	
3rd. Casella-Puccini (Gordini).	12 hr. 05 min. 39 sec.	

Unlimited Sports:

1st. Marzotto-Crosara (Ferrari 4.1).	10 hr. 37 min. 19 sec.	142.347 k.p.h.
		(New record)
2nd. Fangio-Sala (Alfa-Romeo 3.6).		
3rd. Bonetto-Teruzzi (Lancia 2.9).	11 hr. 07 min. 40 sec.	

durability under racing conditions and also appeared to corner in no mean manner. The 1,900 Alfa-Romeos dominated the big touring class, taking the first six places and beating all the Aurelias. Paglini was the winner, though Palmieri led until the last stage of the race. Among the small sports cars the D.B. Panhards proved victors, against strong opposition from numerous Fiat-based specials, Touzot and Persillon winning in their open D.B. None of the Fiats or Cisitalias could hold the beautiful little open Oscas in the 1,100-c.c. Sports Class and Venezian came home the winner at the very high speed of 125.160 k.p.h., while Giletti in the works A6G Maserati won the 2,000-c.c. Class only 4 k.p.h. faster. The big boys really set the records flying, for Giannino Marzotto won at 142.347 k.p.h., which gave him the over-2,000-c.c. Class and made him the outright winner of the whole entry. Such an average over 1,512 kilometres of normal road, much of it of inferior surface and with three mountain passes included, together with traversing over twenty big towns, must surely make the Mille Miglia the Blue Riband of the Sports-Car World. He who wins the Mille Miglia is some driver, and the car he uses is some sports car.

The race for overall victory saw a fierce fight between the British and Italian works teams from Jaguar, Aston Martin, Alfa Romeo, Lancia and Ferrari. The dispute was narrowed down to the Italian marques and the inspired drivers of the Alfa 3000 CM dominated the race until they were delayed by mechanical problems. Overall victory went to Giannino Marzotto and Marco Crosara with the Ferrari 340 MM Vignale (1) at the remarkable average speed of 142.547 kph over the 1,512 km of the race. Juan Manuel Fangio and Giulio Sala with the Alfa Romeo 3000 Cm (2) were second at an average speed of 139.774 kph. The latter had been first to Florence and with 1,171 km completed they were racing at an average speed of over 142 kph and led Marzotto by over 2 minutes. They were delayed with steering problems once past Florence. Felice Bonetto and Presuzzi with the Lancia D 20 (3) were third at an average speed of over 135 kph, leading home the Ferrari 340 MM Vignale (4) of Tom Cole and Mario Vandelli and the Aston Martin DB 3 (5) of Reg Parnell and Louis Klementasky by almost 13 minutes.

4   5

1

69

The Renault 4 CV continued to dominate the 750 cc class of the Turismo Internazionale category, with Adriano Angelelli and M. Recchi (1) completing the race at an average speed of almost 96 kph. The organisers created a sub-class for cars of up to 600 cc for the Italian competitors driving Fiat Topolinos. The sub-class was won by the Fiat 500 C of Sandrolini and Brighenti (2) behind two Renault 4 CVs and seven Dyna Panhards.

In the sub-class for cars of up to 1500 cc, practically reserved for the Fiat 1400, victory went to Massi Benedetti-Bonanno (5) whilst the over 2000 cc class was won by Paul Frère and A. Milhoux with this Chrysler Saratoga (6)

6

The Italian cars gained revenge over their French rivals in the 1300 cc class in which the Fiat 1100/103 (3) of the Mancini brothers easily defeated the Peugeots. With the works Lancia Aurelia B 22s withdrawn in protest against the alleged non-conformity of the Alfa Romeo 1900 TI, the race was a walk-over for the Portello cars, victory going to Pagliai and Parducci (4) at an average of over 120 kph. The pair also took the Turismo Internazionale category title and finished 22nd overall.

4

3

The production sports car category was dominated by foreign marques. Victory in the 750 cc class went to Jean Redelé and Louis Pons in the Renault 4 CV 1063 41) at an average speed of 99.164 kph. Von Hoesch and Hengel took the 1300 cc class with the Porsche 1300 super (2).

1

3

Victory in the 1500 cc class went to the works Porsche 1500 Super (3) of Hans Hermann and Hans Bauer at an average speed of 118 kph. They also won the category overall.

2

In the Sport Internazionale category the DB Panhard (4) of Touzot and Persillon underlined the superiority of the French cars in the small-engined classes. Bruno Venezian and Albarelli with their OSCA Mt4 2AD (5) established an excellent average speed of 125.160 kph, finishing 12th overall and winning the Index of Performance that was officially introduced in 1953 in the wake of its success at Le Mans.

4

6

The 2000 cc Sport Internazionale class was won by the Maserati A6GCS (6) of Emilio Gioletti and Guarino Bertocchi, sixth overall at an average speed of over 129 kph.

5

ASCARI BRINGS VICTORY TO LANCIA IN MILLE MIGLIA

Great Battle Between Ferrari and Lancia. Aston Martins Retire After Being Well Up

Ascari (Lancia) 1953 World's Champion, won the classic Mille Miglia in its 21st year 86.69 m.p.h., slightly slower than last year on account of bad weather on the mountains between Rome and the finish. After a battle in which the Lancias led the Ferraris from the start Taruffi led the race for Lancia as far as Rome and then fell back...engine trouble. The two Aston Martins held high places but were eliminated after half-distance. And, after the first car went out, it was left to the 2-litre class to come up into the general category behind Ascari.
From Grande Vitesse,

Brescia, Sunday Night

The 100 bells of Brescia were swinging their curiously attractive hazard chimes into the growing light when the first of the Unlimited Sports Car class - Piazza's saloon Ferrari plunged down the launching ramp in the Viale Venezia and took the road to Verona. A thin drizzle of rain came with the morning light but ceased as the day grew brighter. The race start-ed with the small touring cars at 9 p.m. on Saturday, led - very temporarily - by a buzzing covey of little Iso "bubble cars," looking like enlarged garden cloches on wheels.

Thereafter, all through the night into the morning the 450-odd cars went off one by one - modified 750 c.c. tourers, 750 c.c. sports cars, modified 1,300 c.c. tourers, 1,500 c.c. Grand Touring cars, over 1,300 c.c. modified tourers, 1,500 c.c. sports, over 1,500 c.c. Grand Tourers, 2-litre sports and over 2-litre sports, in that sequence, calculated so that the order of the race would become almost certainly the actual order of finishing. There was much consternation before the event in the Austin-Healey camp when the organizers transferred them from the Grand Touring class to the out-and-out sports-car unlimited c.c. class. Hasty work removed the new plastic hardtops and converted them back to open two-seaters; Donald Healey withdrew and the team became Chiron, Macklin and Wisdom.

This year for the first time the faster cars were not obliged to convey two occupants. Chiron and Macklin therefore drove so-lo, Wisdom took Morris-Goodall. The Aston Martin team went in pairs - Parnell with Klemantaski, Collins with Griffith - on the latest DB3S cars emitting a very pleasing crackle. Taruffi (3.3 V-6 Lancia), Ascari (ditto) and Anselmi (ditto, saloon) drove alone. Thus, with decked-in passenger seat, the cars looked, sounded and went more like Grand Prix machines than ever. George Abecassis drove the H.W.M.-Jaguar, passengered by what the programme called "Feukinsow" and turned out to be Jenkinson, setting off last of all at 13 minutes past six on Sunday morning.

The remainder of the British entry - lacking Jaguars this year - was a trio of Triumph TR2s, Gatsonides with Richardson, Stoddart and White, and Leslie Brooke and Fairman; Tom Meyer's Aston Martin DB3 coupé; the Swedish driver Nottorp's Frazer-Nash Le Mans coupé; and two foreign-entered Jaguar XK120s in the Grand Touring

The Lancia team in Piazza della Vittoria. The D 24s of Alberto Ascari (no. 602) and Gino Valenzano (no. 541) can be seen.

class, one the hardtop coupé of rally driver Gendebien fresh from his co-victory in the Tulip Rally. Top weight in the entry list were the latest 4.9 Mondial Ferrari two-seaters (Maglioli, P. Marzotto and Farina) against the 3.3 Lancia Aurelias led by Ascari and Taruffi. One new 6-cylinder, 3-litre Maserati also ran (Mantovani).

There were 26 1.500 c.c. sports cars, 26 2-litres and 31 over 2-litres in the total field of 380 starters - much smaller than last year.

Hemmed-in

If the entry was reduced, the enthusiasm was not. I watched the passage of the cars about 10 miles outside Brescia in a village with a level crossing and a fast curve.

Thousands of people lined both sides of the road, standing in the gutters and sitting on the kerbs three and four deep, so close that they moved back as the cars went past and, finding that I was being buffeted by the wind of their passage and that I was so close that I could have touched the drivers.

I thought discretion the better part of spectating and withdrew. Police blew whistles, the crowd buzzed with excitement, pressing forward to watch the approaching dot swelling into a car moving at 140 m.p.h., frantically waving handkerchiefs at their favourites, swaying back as the cars shot past and swaying out again to see the cars dwindle to a whining dot again in the distance, and then breaking out into a roar of excited comment. Of all who passed, Taruffi looked fastest, taking the bends almost flat with one quick lift of the foot in third gear and a long power-slide.

Ascari was more sedate, Farina fighting his wheel. On the first 40 miles, Taruffi averaged 115.8 m.p.h. - 26 seconds faster than Ascari. The roads were dry, the day growing brighter but with heavy cloud looming.

Farina Injured

Within an hour news came of the first crash, French driver Bouschol (Citroen) hit a telegraph pole near Firenze and, it was reported, injured eight of the crowd, and he and his co-driver were taken to hospital.

Then came news that Farina had left the road near Lake Garda, breaking an arm.

It was already obvious that, barring rain, records were going to be broken, Lesur (Renault) reached Rome over half an hour before the big cars started running, in the 750 c.c. class, and the class was led by Redele, also driving a Renault, at 68.2 m.p.h. - almost 7 m.p.h. faster than the 1953 class average. Right from the start Taruffi led the race in the 3.3 Lancia, drawing gradually away from an unusually cautious Ascari.

At Ferrara, Taruffi led at 114.9 m.p.h. An astonishing average through towns and villages, over bridges and level crossings, and through those appalling crowds lining the streets. Ascari lay second, 3 min. 58 sec. behind, and Maglioli's 4.9 Ferrari, third, 2 sec. behind Ascari, Gendebien's Jaguar led the big touring class. Mantovani, in the large Maserati, retired and there were two more crashes Cestelli's Alfa Romeo and Lautenschlager's Porsche. At Ravenna, a quarter of the way, Castellotti passed Maglioli,

putting three Lancias in the lead - 1, Taruffi, 109.3 m.p.h. 2, Ascari, closing up with 1 min. 38 sec. 3, Castellotti. 4, Maglioli (Ferrari). 5, P. Marzotto (4.9 Ferrari). 6, his brother, G. Marzotto (1953 winner) (4.9 Ferrari). 7, Valenzano (Lancia). 8, P. Collins (Aston Martin). 9, Bordoni (2.3 Gordini). 10, Reg Parnell (Aston Martin).

Last year's average, by Sanesi (Alfa Romeo), 108.5 m.p.h.

At Pescara, after the long full-throttle straight down the Adriatic coast, Ascari closed in slightly but Taruffi still led at 109 m.p.h., Valenzano (Lancia) passed Marzotto (Ferrari) but blew up very soon afterwards, and Parnell passed Collins into seventh place. Scotti's Ferrari 8th and Collins 9th. Macklin and Wisdom (Austin-Healeys) 18 and 19 in the class.

A terrific duel was developing now in the 2-litre sports-car class between V.Marzotto (2-litre Ferrari) and Musso (Maserati), in which Marzotto led at 99 m.p.h. and lay 8th in the general category irrespective of engine size. Chiron on the third Austin-Healey gave up on account of a broken brake-pipe.

Retirements were coming thick and fast but, so far, the high-speed brigade was not affected. The German Hermann, on the latest two-seater open Porsche with four overhead camshafts, led the 1,500 c.c. sports-car class by a quarter of an hour, and was rapidly coming into the picture in the general category. Now among the Abruzzi mountains on the way to Rome, Taruffi's oil pressure began to flicker but, driving at terrific speed, he came into the Rome control

leading Ascari by 4 1/2 minutes and then stopped to rectify the fault and lost the best part of an hour, and Ascari shot off into the lead on the return half of the long race which has always been the decisive stage. It is a maxim: Who leads at Rome loses the Mille Miglia, which has always been true.

Castellotti disappeared, Maglioli was third, P.Marzotto fourth, Parnell went off the road and out of the race, Collins took fifth place and up came the 2-litre cars - V. Marzotto (Ferrari) and Musso (Maserati), still battling away madly, a few seconds apart.

At Florence, Ascari led by over five minutes at 86 m.p.h.

As the sky darkend and rain poured down, P. Marzotto was in 2nd place, Maglioli 3rd, and Scotti 4th. Across the River Arno they stormed, and wended their way up the Futa Pass over the Appenine backbone of Italy and P. Marzotto gave up with an unserviceable gearbox.

And his amazing brother with the
2-litre Ferrari came into second
place with Musso's Maserati third
and 4 sec. behind. At this stage
of the race, Wisdom (Austin-
Healey) retired with a broken radiator hose, leaving Macklin alone,
fifth in his class.

The second Aston Martin, driven
by Collins, retired after the Rome
control, Brooke on the Triumph,
ran out of fuel and Meyer's Aston
Martin coupé went off the road.
Now on the last stage through
Cremona and Mantua, a detour
this year in honour of Nuvolari,
Ascari led with half an hour in
hand, but now the 2-litre cars had
come into the picture and, in sixth
place, was the ultra-lightweight
Porsche of Hermann in the 1,500
c.c. sports class.

At the finish, Ascari rushed over
the line to win his first Mille Miglia
by nearly four minutes, V. Marzotto was second, with Musso
(Maserati) only 9 sec. behind after
12 hours' racing, Biondetti (2.9
Ferrari) fourth and then Venezian
on the under 2-litre Maserati.

Motor Sport, June, 1954

XXIst 1000 MIGLIA

Victory for Ascari and Lancia Under Poor Conditions

The Frazer Nash Le Mans of Nottorp and Brant, 53rd overall at the finish.

BRESCIA, May 3rd.

For a whole week before the XXIst Mille Miglia Northern Italy was under a continuous deluge of rain and some of the enthusiasm in Brescia was lacking a little, but, having seen a Mille Miglia under perfect conditions, this slight lessening in the tumult made life easier. With an entry of 475 cars, ranging from 2 c.v. Citroëns to 4.9-litre Ferraris, it can be appreciated that competition in the various classes was enormous. Naturally, the battle for the Franco Mazzotti Cup, the prize for the outright winner, was confined to the sports class for cars over 2,000 c.c., and this year the chief protagonists were Ferrari and Lancia. Both factories threw in all they had, the Rampant Horse being upheld by Farina, Gianni Marzotto, Paolo Marzotto and Maglioli, all with open two-seater 4.9-litre Ferraris. This year, for the first time in the Mille Miglia, any sports car over 750 c.c. capacity was not obliged to carry a passenger, but of the big Ferraris only Maglioli went solo, his car having a fairing over the passenger's seat and a large streamlined headrest behind his own seat. There was also a curious multitude of aero-screens and wind-deflectors, and his car

looked far more purposeful than many Grand Prix cars. Piero Scotti was lent an open two-seater 4.5-litre Ferrari by the factory and Biondetti had a similar 3-litre. The Lancia team consisted of four 3.3-litre cars, similar to those used in the Pan-American and the recent Sebring race; all were running without passengers, and also looked very fine Grand Prix cars. They were driven by Ascari, Taruffi, Castellotti and Valenzano, while a fifth car was brought along to the scrutineering on the Friday before the race. This one should have been driven by Villoresi, but he was still insufficiently recovered from the accident he met with during some practising when his mechanic was driving.

Although the whole Lancia team were running as single-seaters they still had to have provision for carrying a passenger and at the scrutineering Renzo Castagneto, the organiser, insisted on seeing a car with the cockpit cover removed and a mechanic and driver sitting in the car. It was perfectly satisfactory and, amid cheers and laughter, he clasped young Gianni Lancia warmly by the hand and everyone was happy. In addition to the four open cars Lancias entered Piodi and Anselmi with special 2.5-litre Aurelias, the former in one of the red cars used last year at Monza and the latter with a blue and cream one used by Claes to win the Liège-Rome-Liège Rally.

Supporting the factory Ferraris were an impressive team entered by the Scuderia Guastalla, under the organization of Franco Cornacchia, the Milan Ferrari agent. Musitelli and Pezzoli had open two-seaters and Signorina Piazza and Gerini had Farina coupés, all on the new 3-litre V12 chassis. A lone Maserati from the factory was in this class, being a hurriedly prepared two-seater version of the new 2-litre Formula I car, with de Dion rear axle and everything. This was driven by Mantovani. Another lone entry was a 3-litre Gordini driven by Bordoni under the watchful eye of the "sorcerer" himself, but being painted red and run as an Italian entry. Against all these cars were pit-

The Triumph TR2 of Stoddart and White at the start.

ted a collection of English cars led by the two workmanlike 3-litre Aston Martins driven by Parnell and Collins. They had been practising and testing for some weeks beforehand and made worthy representatives of the Union Jack. They were not modified in any serious way from last year's cars, being the DB3S models, now with outboard rear brakes, and having nicely moulded Perspex windshields and the passenger's side of the cockpit enclosed as much as space would permit. There was a privately entered DB3 Aston Martin belonging to Meyer, the coupé body having been lowered and smoothed out since last year, and a lone H.W.M. driven by Abecassis, this car being fitted with a Jaguar XK engine and gearbox, the chassis being comprised of Formula II parts, having transverse leaf-spring and wishbone i.f.s. and de Dion rear axle on torsion-bars. Also in this formidable class were the Austin-Healey team; they had entered for the Grand Turismo class with three cars built around the production two-seater body but fitted with bolted-on "hard-tops" of the type produced in quantity for normal Jaguars, M.G.s and suchlike. None of the cars were accepted by the scrutineers as regulations for the Gran Turismo class were very strict and every detail had to conform with a catalogue sent in with the entry. It

was this paperwork detail that Healeys had overlooked and no one was prepared to believe that the cars were standard production models. As a result they were transferred to the "big boys" class and those of Macklin and Chiron were run as single-seaters with cockpit fairings and small Perspex windscreens, while Wisdom took a passenger. All three cars were fitted with Dunlop disc brakes and new Dunlop magnesium disc wheels that were located by the five dowel pins, the wheel being held in place by a three-eared knock-off hub nut. The 2.6-litre Austin engines were the normal power plants, fitted with twin S.U. carburetters fed by an airduct from the front of the car, and a double-pipe exhaust system rejected from the side of the cars just in front of the off-side rear wheel. Four-speed gearboxes, manufactured for Austins by David Brown, were fitted, with central remote control. The

whole of the boot was occupied by a 32-gallon fuel tank, with a large filler protruding through the lid. Considering that the cars had been prepared from standard production models they looked most effective but were severely handicapped by being a half litre down on the average of competitors in the class. From the foregoing imposing list of cars and drivers the winner of the XXIst Mille Miglia was expected and Maglioli and Taruffi were hot favourites. Hard on the heels of the big class was the 1,500 to 2,000-c.c. class and here the battle for honours was between Maserati and Ferrari. Maseratis were running one official car, but as the 2-litre sports car is now being produced in numbers the others were prepared by the factory for the new owners, some of them being delivered just before the race. Musso was the number one driver and the other Maseratis were driven by Mancini (with the

special Vignale-bodied car), Venezian, Scarlatti, Bertoni, Bosisio and Cacciari; the last five being in standard production two-seater A6G models. Strong opposition to the six-cylinder cars was coming from Ferrari with four Mondial models, the new four-cylinder 2-litre on a chassis developed from the Formula II cars, with de Dion axle and four-speed gearboxes. Sterzi, Neri and Vittorio Marzotto had factory cars, the last named having the prototype with normal rear axle. A fourth Mondial was that of Cortese, entered by the Scuderia Guastalia and both his and Marzotto's car were running without passengers and with cockpit fairings and small aeroscreens, the latter also having a head-fairing. Sanesi had a 1,900C Alfa-Romeo, nicely described as a Supersprint model, meaning that it looked standard but wasn't quite. A Swedish driver, Nottorp, was running a brand new Frazer-Nash Le

Mans coupé, painted Italian red, and Piotti had a 2-litre Osca, being similar to the normal sports Osca but fitted with a six-cylinder Formula II type of engine. Looking rather lost amongst all this fierce machinery were three TR2 Triumphs driven by Gatsonides, Stoddart, and the third shared by Brooke and Fairman.

The 750-1,500-c.c. class, which in all such events is usually the playground of Osca, was this time being severely challenged by the young German driver Hermann with a factory Porsche. This was the open two-seater with the four-overhead camshaft engine fitted in front of the rear axle. Cabianca was upholding Osca fortunes with some private owners backing him up. The rest of the 475 entries came from a mass of tiny sports cars in the up-to-750-c.c. class, with a good entry of French teams pitting open two-seater D.B. Pan-

hards and Renaults against local drivers with Fiat Specials, Stanguellinis, Giaurs, Siatas and one-off specials. Naturally a big proportion of the entries was made up by the Special Series Touring categories in which almost anything could be done to the mechanical details of the car providing the outside appearance was not altered. The removal of the radiator grille from a baby Fiat could cause disqualification, but two huge carburetters, a special inlet manifold and tuned exhaust manifold were allowable. Divided into capacity groups the touring cars provided some lively competition: Panhard, Renault and Fiat battling with less than 750 c.c., more than 90 Fiat 1,100 models being opposed by lonely D.K.W. Lancia Appia and Peugeot entries in the class up to 1,300 c.c., and 1,900 Alfa-Romeos dominating the over-1,300-c.c. class. In the

same way, Lancia Aurelias dominated the over-1,500-c.c. Gran Turismo class and Porsches the same group under 1,500 c.c. As light relief to all this serious motoring that was about to take place, 20th Century Fox Films were about the place making scenes for the film production of Hans Ruesch's book "The Racer". Two cars were officially entered for the Mille Miglia, one a 2-litre Ferrari two-seater, the other a 2-litre Burano, this actually being an early 2-litre Ferrari with a modified body - so well done that many people spent a long time puzzling over the origin of the car. This was driven by the American driver Fitch and the other car by de Graffenried and, keeping out of the way of the race itself, they were all set to race against each other for a few miles after the start, before withdrawing.

As is traditional, the small cars

began leaving Brescia at minute intervals from 9 p.m. on Saturday evening, May 1st, the first competitor's number being 2,100. All through the night cars left the starting ramp places in the middle of the main road out of Brescia to the east, and as the hours passed so the cars got faster and noisier and the crowds bigger and more excited. Dawn was breaking as the first Maserati went off the line with an ear-splitting roar from its exhaust, and it was daylight by the time the big factory cars left. The noise and tumult as the Marzotto brothers roared off and then Maglioli, Taruffi, Biondetti, Ascari, Farina and the rest got away was unbelievable. Last to leave was Abecassis in the H.W.M. and that was 6.13 a.m., by which time news was coming in from points along the course.

To the first big town, Verona, the top drivers were averaging over 115 m.p.h. and the pace was fantastic bearing in mind there were 1,597 kilometres (approximately 1,000 miles) to cover. The battle of the giants was well and truly under way, but equally the battles in the various classes were just as fierce. In a race the size and magnitude of the Mille Miglia the outright winner is obviously the hero of the day and all over Italy eyes were on these fantastic "sports cars" that are as fast as current Grand Prix cars. Impressionable people were speaking of 192 m.p.h. for the

Lance Macklin was one of the first to tackle the exhausting race without a co-driver in this Austin Healey 100. He finished 23rd overall.

big Ferraris, for they had said last year that the 4-litres were doing 185 m.p.h. However, Lancias, with only 3.3 litres, were never being given a maximum speed, but they could clearly do over 150 m.p.h., probably 155, so if we settle for 160 m.p.h. for the 4.9-litre Ferrari we shall not be far out, especially as Taruffi made fastest average on the initial 40-mile "blind" from Brescia to Verona. The Lancia unquestionably has better roadholding than the Ferrari, which would explain this anomaly.

During the 1,597 kilometres there were control points in eight big towns, at which the driver had to stop and have his route card stamped, while at Rome and Bologna he also had to have a punch mark made in a fibre disc attached to the steering column. None of these stops necessitated being stationary for more than five seconds, for the speed and enthusiasm of the marshals at the controls was superb; in fact, the whole organisation behind the Mille Miglia is one of enormous enthusiasm and these control marshals personify the Mille Miglia spirit. At Ravenna Taruffi was leading by 1 min. 38 sec. from Ascari and 2 min. 47 sec. from Maglioli, followed by Castellotti, and Paolo Marzotto, so now the situation was clear. In spite of Ferraris 4.9 litres the Lancia team was first, second and fourth, and at the next control, Pescara, the Lancias were

first, second and third in front of Maglioli, with Valenzano fifth, and this on the fastest section of the course, Taruffi's leading average being 177.257 k.p.h. (over 109 m.p.h.). Farina had gone off the road very shortly after the start, wrecking the Ferrari completely and suffering a broken arm and damaged face, while Giannino Marzotto withdrew after 400 kilometres of racing, almost admitting that the 4.9-litre Ferrari was more than he was prepared to cope with. At Aquila, after some mountain driving, the order of the first two was unchanged, with Taruffi leading Ascari by four minutes. Castellotti and Valenzano were both out with mechanical trouble, and Maglioli and Paolo Marzotto, the baby of the family, were third and fourth.
Taruffi reached Rome in 5 hr. 30 min. 19 sec., at which point the course turns north and heads back up the Apennine chain to Bologna and Brescia; he was still

leading Ascari by over four minutes and Maglioli by more than 11 minutes. At this point Collins in the Aston Martin arrived in fifth place, driving hard and gaining places as the more powerful cars fell out, and he was just over 38 minutes behind Taruffi. In the other classes competition was enormous and Vittorio Marzotto, with the 2-litre Ferrari, was leading Musso by only 12 seconds. Hermann was well on form, having 15 minutes in hand over Cabianca, but in the touring class Carini was leading Dalla Favera by only 17 seconds, their 1,900 Alfa-Romeo saloons being driven at the limit the whole way. Many had fallen by the wayside and among those who did it literally was Parnell, who smashed his Aston Martin completely when he ran off the road on a fast bend near Popoli. Neither he nor his passenger, Klemantaski, were hurt, but the left front wheel and suspension was torn from

the chassis, engine crankcase and gearbox shells were split and the chassis frame broken; in fact, a write-off. Others who were out were Chiron with a broken brake pipe on his Austin-Healey and Abecassis with a broken shock-absorber and a recalcitrant engine, while Meyer had spun off the road. The 2-litre Maserati had been too hurriedly prepared and lasted only a few miles, and both factory Aurelias were out. Clearly the pace was too fast and it was a matter of the survival of the fittest, and doubts began to be raised as to whether anyone would survive, for after Rome the Mille Miglia really gets tough with the crossing of the mountain passes. The recent severe winter had played havoc with the roads of Italy and they were in a terribly rough condition, and averaging 100 m.p.h. on such roads was taking its toll. This was not a race round a billiard-table-surfaced track, it was

81

high speed on everyday roads that you had to take as you found, pot-holes, bumps, gravel surfaces, road construction, level crossings, cobble stones and every imaginable hazard being all part of the course, and if any car was going to survive it would have to be very fit.

From Rome the mountain passes showed the point of the 4.9-litre Ferrari engines, for both Maglioli and Paolo Marzotto began to eat up the minutes they were behind the Lancias. In none of the previous Mille Miglias that have been run has the leader at Rome ever been the winner of the race. On all occasions he was either beaten on the mountain stretch or had to retire. The 1954 Mille Miglia was no exception for on the stretch to Siena Taruffi had an accident while overtaking another competitor and left the road, breaking an oil pipe in the process. Although he was able to limp to Florence all hope of winning was gone and he had to retire. This left Ascari now in the lead, much

to the delight of the Italian public and Maglioli and Marzotto were now pressing hard, using all the might of 4.9-litre engine as they stormed up the Radicofani Pass. By Siena Ascari had only 53 seconds lead over Maglioli and 1 min. 52 sec. lead over Marzotto, both of these young drivers now putting all they had into their driving. Scotti had now come up into fourth place, with Vittorio Marzotto, doing a fantastic drive in the 2-litre Ferrari, now in fifth place and leading Musso by 1 minutes. Collins, in the remaining Aston Martin, was a splendid sixth only seconds behind Vittorio Marzotto. From Siena to Florence the excitement grew, for Paolo Marzotto made up a minute on Maglioli and was lying second at the control, but Ascari had had something in reserve and had drawn away a bit. The order was now Ascari, having been driving for 8 hr. 22 min. 18 sec., second Paolo Marzotto, third Maglioli, fourth Scotti, then Musso and Vittorio Marzotto in the 2-litre cars lying fifth and

sixth, respectively, only one second apart, and Collins seventh. The reason for the Aston Martin's demise was that it had run off the road and bent the rear end and broken an engine bearer, so that the prop-shaft resting on a cross-member was all that was holding the engine in the car. Collins managed to limp in to Florence but there had to retire after a very good drive.

Now came an important part of the race, the traversing of the Raticosa and Futa passes in quick succession between Florence and Bologna, and it looked as though the power of the Ferraris was going to show. Apart from the battle for the lead there was also the struggle in the 2-litre class between Musso and Marzotto, so that at Bologna news from the mountains was awaited with tension. All the important cars were reported as having started the mountain section and when, just over one hour later, Ascari arrived at the control at Bologna it was clear that both Ferraris were in trouble.

Ascari's number was 602, Marzotto's 536 and Maglioli's 545, so both Ferraris should have arrived before the Lancia. After refuelling Ascari literally toured away, firm in the knowledge that he had only to finish to win. Up in the mountains Maglioli had run off the road and damaged the car too badly to continue and Marzotto had broken his gearbox so that the last of the opposition was gone. The 2-litre cars, however, were still going strongly and Vittorio Marzotto was 1 min. 18 sec. in front of Musso with the last high-speed stage in front of them. Biondetti was now fourth, a long way back and looking very tired, and Scotti had an enormous accident all by himself and smashed up both ends of the 4-litre Ferrari, but managed to limp along to the Bologna control where he retired. The General Category of the XXIst Mille Miglia had now fizzled out, Ascari was touring in to win after a very hard race, his average speed dropping to below last year's record, even though the pace had been much harder. All interest was now on the 2-litre category and the battle between Marzotto and Musso which was so close as to seem impossible after such a distance of racing. At Mantova, the course being deviated from previous years to pass through the home town of Nuvolari in homage to that "great little man," they were still only seconds apart and right to the very last of the 1,597 kilometres

both drivers were going all they knew, passing through the outskirts of Brescia, and over the finishing line as if on the first lap of a Grand Prix. Musso was the first to arrive, his starting time having been 5 a.m. and Marzotto arrived some 23 minutes later, his number being 523. The timekeepers did their sums and Vittorio Marzotto had won by 9 sec. after racing for 12 hours and this put him second in General Category with Musso third.

The whole race had been one of mechanical massacre, brought about partly by the furious pace set at the beginning and partly by the conditions of the roads which were worse than has been seen for many years. The weather did not improve matters, for though race day was not as wet as the previous week, conditions were always changing from fog, rain, and clouds to hot sunshine and it was a very tired and dirty Alberto Ascari that won his first Mille Miglia and Lancia's first victory in this toughest of all sports-car races. As remarked

last year, he who wins the Mille Miglia is some driver, and the car he uses is some sports car!

MILLE MIGLIA MUSINGS

In an event the size of the Mille Miglia it is not possible to mention every praiseworthy effort, but one that was particularly good was that of the Belgian driver Gendebien who won the Tulip Rally, flew to Italy and drove a Jaguar XK120 coupé into 21st place. Likewise, Gatsonides competed in the Tulip Rally and the Mille Miglia, finishing 28th with a Triumph TR2.

The first British car to finish was the Austin-Healey driven by Macklin, who drove on his own and likened the event to a one-lap Grand Prix of interminable length, but more interesting than covering lap after lap of the same circuit. He finished in 23rd place and fifth out of the six finishers in his class.

Other English cars to complete the course were a Jaguar coupé, driven by two French drivers, in 37th place, the coupé

Frazer-Nash driven by the Swedish drivers Nottorp and Bratt, in 53rd place, and Brooke and Fairman with the Troumph TR2 in 94th place.

An intrepid couple were the German drivers Strable and Spingler who had a Volkswagen fitted with a Porsche engine, Porsche brakes and wheels. They finished third in the sports class, out of 12 finishers, and 44th in General category, with what must surely have been a very "dicey" hot-rod!

The last car to complete the course was an Isetta, a midget economy saloon balanced on wheel-barrow wheels and powered by a 350-c.c. two-stroke engine, that arrived back at Brescia 24 hr. 37 min. 2 sec. after leaving, but it could not be classified as 24 hours was the maximum time allowed. Seven of these incredible little vehicles

competed, four qualified, and the fastest averaged approximately 45 m.p.h. for the 1,000 miles.

Venezian, who finished fifth in General Category, was indebted to the officials at Bologna, for he arrived at the control too fast, locked his wheels and skidded into one of the grandstands, injuring a small boy and denting the nose of his Maserati. The accident looked serious at first and he seemed prepared to abandon the race, but the officials pushed the car back on the road and sent him on his way before he could really appreciate what had happened.

Unluckiest man was surely Mancini who crashed his Maserati within a few miles of Brescia, his mechanic unfortunately receiving fatal injuries.

It was most impressive at Bologna the way most of the Al-

MILLE MIGLIA Italy 1,597 Kilometres Conditions Poor

* 1st: A. Ascari (Lancia 3.3 litre) 11 hr. 26 min. 10 sec. <- 139.645 k.p.h.
* 2nd: V. Marzotto (Ferrari 2-litre) 12 hr. 0 min. 1 sec. - 133.080 "
  3rd: L. Musso-Zocca (Maserati 2-litre) 12 hr. 0 min. 10 sec. - 133.052 "
  4th: C. Biondetti (Ferrari 3-litre) 12 hr. 15 min. 36 sec. - 130.261 "
  5th: B. Venezian-Orlandi (Maserati 3-litre) 12 hr. 27 min. 43 sec. - 128.436 "
* 6th: H. Hermann-Linge (Porsche 1.5 litre) 12 hr. 35 min. 44 sec. - 126.790 "
* 7th: G. Serafini-Mancini (Lancia Aurelia) 12 hr. 47 min. 12 sec. - 124.895 "
* 8th: P. Carini-Artesani (Alfa-Romeo 1900) 12 hr. 51 min. 52 sec. - 124.140 "
  9th: Leto di Priolo, C and S (Fiat 8V-Zagato) 12 hr. 52 min. 38 sec.
  10th: G. Cabianca (Osca 1.5-litre) 12 hr. 55 min. 8 sec.

Class Results:

750 c.c., Touring:
1st: Rédélé-Pons (Renault) 15 hr. 4 min. 33 sec. - 105.931 k.p.h.
2nd: Galtier-Michy (Renault) 15 hr. 22 min. 40 sec.
3rd: Guarnieri-Brancaleon (Renault) 15 hr. 36 min. 31 sec.
67 starters; 34 finishers.

1,300 c.c., Touring:
1st: Madrini-Ferraris (Fiat 1,100) 14 hr. 30 min. 46 sec. - 110.040 k.p.h.
2nd: Zanetti-Adria (Fiat 1,100) 14 hr. 37 min. 18 sec.
3rd: Perdisa-Masetti (Fiat 1,100) 14 hr. 52 min. 55 sec.
95 starters; 53 finishers.

Over 1,300 c.c., Touring:
1st: Carini-Artesani (Alfa-Romeo 1,900) 12 hr. 57 min. 52 sec. - 124.140 k.p.h.
2nd: Dalla Favera-Artusi (Alfa-Romeo 1,900) 12 hr. 56 min. 10 sec.
3rd: Franceschetti-Meo Polo (Alfa-Romeo 1,900) 13 hr. 38 min. 12 sec.
37 starters; 20 finishers.

Gran Turismo up to 1,500 c.c.:
1st: v. Frankenberg-Sauter (Porsche) 13 hr. 53 min. 50 sec. - 114.915 k.p.h.
2nd: Hampel-v. Trips (Porsche) 14 hr. 11 min. 23 sec.
3rd: Nathan-Glockler (Porsche) 14 hr. 13 min. 14 sec.
20 starters; 13 finishers.

Gran Turismo over 1,500 c.c.:
1st: Serafini-Mancini (Lancia Aurelia) 12 hr. 47 min. 12 sec. - 124.895 k.p.h.
2nd: Leto di Priolo-Leto di Priolo (Fiat 8V Zagato) 12 hr. 52 min. 38 sec.
3rd: Petrobelli-Cremonesi (Lancia Aurelia) 13 hr. 3 min. 42 sec.
26 starters; 16 finishers.

fa-Romeo 1,900 and Lancia Aurelia cars arrived at speed and still had sufficient brakes to leave marks on the road or lock the front wheels. Most of the Alfa-Romeo left in a flurry of wheel-spin. All this after some 10 hours of racing.

An unknown driver received exactly the same speedy attention at the controls as Ascari or Marzotto, the officials merely did their jobs as fast as possible, irrespective of car or driver. At one point four 1,100 Fiats arrived together and they all got away together, less than 10 seconds being lost by any of them. The marshals who did the official stamping and punching of the cards had the remarkable ability of never being upright, they were continually at an angle of 45 deg. either accelerating, braking or cornering round a car.

No. 613 - MILLE MIGLIA BY OUR CONTINENTAL CORRESPONDENT

As the Mille Miglia is a difficult race at which to spectate and a dull one from the Press grandstand, I decided that it would be more interesting to take part in the event. Also it would provide the opportunity of satisfying a schoolboy ambition, to ride as a racing-mechanic in the most fantastic of all races; a desire that was born in the early days of the Ulster T.T. and from photographs of Mille Miglia Alfa-Romeos studied avidly under cover of a history book - the real reason for utter failure in all examinations. Another desire was to sample the 150-m.p.h. speeds that are spoken of lightly by people "in the know" these days. Not long ago it was 100 m.p.h., but now you do that with all the family on board and a sports car must do 150 m.p.h. So I was prepared to try it, not just up the by-pass, but in the Mille Miglia. By a sequence of coincidences and misunderstandings I finally settled to ride with George Abecassis in the H.W.M.-Jaguar, a motor car in the true sporting tradition, no frills, no sleek coupé top, but a blood-and-thunder sports car of this present age. Independent front suspension with transverse leaf-spring and wishbones, tubular chassis frame, de Dion rear suspension on torsion-bars,

Sports up to 750 c.c.:

1st: Faure-Storez (D. B. Panhard) 15 hr. 3 min. 16 sec. - 106.081 k.p.h.

2nd: Stempert-Schwarz (D. B. Panhard) 15 hr. 53 min. 15 sec.

3rd: Gignoux-Beauce (D. B. Panhard) 16 hr. 21 min. 40 sec.

46 starters; 14 finishers.

Sports up to 1,500 c.c.:

1st: Hermann-Linge (Porsche) 12 hr. 35 min. 44 sec. - 126.790 k.p.h.

2nd: Cabianca (Osca) 12 hr. 55 min. 8 sec.

3rd: Strahle-Spingler (Volkswagen Special) 14 hr. 34 min. 35 sec.

26 starters; 12 finishers.

Sports up to 2,000 c.c.:

1st: V. Marzotto (Ferrari) 12 hr. 0 min. 1 sec. - 133.080 k.p.h.

2nd: Musso-Zocca (Maserati) 12 hr. 0 min. 10 sec.

3rd: Venezian-Orlandi (Maserati) 12 hr. 27 min. 43 sec.

26 starters; 12 finishers.

Sports over 2,000 c.c.:

1st: Ascari (Lancia) 11 hr. 26 min. 10 sec. - 139.645 k.p.h.

2nd: Biondetti (Ferrari) 12 hr. 15 min. 36 sec.

3rd: Minzoni-Brinci (Ferrari) 13 hr. 10 min. 34 sec.

31 starters; 6 finishers.

Total starters, 374; total finishers, 180.

G.P. of Nuvolari (fastest time Cremona-Mantova-Brescia - 134 kilometres):
Ascari (Lancia), 44 min. 4.8 sec. - 180.353 k.p.h.

position of the gear lever, for 4,500 r.p.m. in top meant 120 m.p.h. as the car was geared for 26.9 m.p.h. per 1,000 revs. in top gear. Having never travelled at more than a genuine 110 m.p.h. on the road before, I Viewed "4,500" with interest, but could not help taking a rather blasé view of the speed. Then the needle went up to 5,000 and on up to 5,400 r.p.m. - that was different; I was very conscious of being in a realm about which I had no experience and the feeling was odd to say the least, and I began to pay very close attention to all about me. Then

brakes from the Formula II cars and an all-enveloping body topped by a curved Perspex windshield. The cockpit was spacious and the closely-fitting bucket-seats allowed one to see just over the windshield but not in the air-stream.

Meeting the H.W.M. equipe in Brescia a few details were added, such as drinking bottles with long rubber pipes, a bracket made to keep a tin of sweets and some oranges in place, a block of wood on the floor for me to brace my feet against, a little "bungy" rubber padding, a second handhold on the tail of the car, and we were then ready for a trial run on the Autostrada. The only indication of speed was the large rev.-counter and the

some traffic appeared and we were back to a cruising 100 m.p.h. Yes, I was quite certain I was going to enjoy the Mille Miglia.

Dawn had broken and a dull grey sky was overhead as the over-2-litre sports class lined up on the main road out of Brescia, and above the general clamour I could occasionally hear the rasp of a racing engine and the rising crescendo as a Ferrari or Lancia roared away towards Verona. We were last in the row of cars; when we had gone, at 6.13 a.m., the organisers could go and have breakfast and the crowds go to sleep. In front of us was Tom Meyer's light green Aston Martin coupé, and as he mounted the starting ramp and was given the signal to start I set my watch to 6.12 and then we drove up onto the ramp, surrounded by a sea of cheering faces and waving hands. An official gave me our control card that had to be stamped eight times during the next 1,000 miles. Castagneto and Count Maggi, the two most important men in Brescia, the real brains behind the Mille Miglia, were there smiling, and it was 6.13 and we were away. Gently down the ramp and then accelerating away through the gears. In front of us was a solid block of people but Abecassis had done many Mille Miglia and he just drove

straight at them with the speed rising to 80 and 90 m.p.h. When they were petrifyingly close the crowd swayed back to let us pass, and for the next 20 or 30 miles it seemed that we must sweep them down by the hundred, but they always moved aside in time. The greatest difficulty was that it was quite impossible to see any of the corners or bends because the crowds covered everything, and I thought how infuriating it must be to learn the course on a normal day and then try to remember it under these conditions. Everyone had had the same trouble, for the number of marks on the road from panic-braking were unbelievable, and every corner showed signs of one of the 373 cars in front of us having had a

dodgy moment, with black marks up onto pavements, signs of locking wheels, and so on. Once clear of Brescia the road straightened up and "5,000" and more was showing on the rev.-counter in top as commonly as the average cars shows 50 m.p.h. on its speedometer. It was not long before we saw a speck in the distance, that was number 612 and at nearly 130 m.p.h. he went past; by now the crowds were thinning out, though the villages and towns were still packed. In Peschiera the crowd were nearly delirious and their attempts to slow us down were fascinating, one man even running straight at us waving a chair. Round the next corner we saw the reason for all this pandemonium. No. 606 was

well and truly wrapped round a tree and a quick look at the list stuck on our dashboard showed it to be Farina. I exchanged a wry look with Abecassis just before he opened out and we got back into our 130-m.p.h. stride. Out of Verona the road ran dead straight but was lined with people, most of whom seemed to have bicycles or umbrellas, and at 140 m.p.h. we drove through this sea of "ants" with only a three-foot space on each side of the car, the only consolation being that they were all interested in the Mille Miglia and were probably looking towards us. On 120-m.p.h. bends in the open country there would still be a crowd of people standing right on the apex, exactly at the point where a car would leave the road, presumably all quite oblivious of the danger. Once away from Verona "5,200" came up and after a while I had the feeling of being satisfied with having done 142 m.p.h. on the open road and was quite prepared for Abecassis to ease back to a sedate 100 m.p.h., but as far as the eye could see the road ran straight and was completely clear, so there was no reason to ease off and for mile after mile we cruised at 142 m.p.h. Eventually a blind brow necessitated the throttle being eased back and the speed dropped to around 120 m.p.h., but only for a fleeting moment

Vittorio Marzotto, at the wheel of the Ferrari 500 Mondial Scaglietti (2) saved Maranello's honour by finishing second overall and winning the two-litre Sport Internazionale class from the Maserati A6GCSs of Luigi Musso and Zocca (3rd overall, photo 3) and Bruno Venezian and Orlandi (5th overall, photo 4). The talented Vicenza driver also won the Nuvolari GP on the Cremona-Mantua-Brescia section at an average speed of 177.579 kph. Clemente Biondetti driving this Ferrari 2500 MM bodied by Morelli of Ferrara (1) finished fourth overall.

and we were back to our maximum again with nothing but straight flat road in front of us. In Vicenza the road was very bad and on one corner we hit a bump which threw us almost onto the pavement, the crowd stepping smartly backwards as one man. Out of the town we accelerated up to three figures and soon realised something was wrong for the car was wandering about at over 120 m.p.h. and clearly the big bump in Vicenza had broken something, probably a shock-absorber or part of the rear suspension, for on corners

the car was behaving most peculiarly. After a time we became used to the snaking above 120 m.p.h. and as there was no one immediately in front of us we had all the road to play with. We had caught 612, 611 did not start, and 610 we had seen by the roadside a long way back. No. 609 was Peter Collins with the works Aston Martin and, now that we could not corner very fast, obviously we could not catch him.

After Padova a thick mist developed which reduced visibility to less than 100 yards and limited

speed to a bare 100 m.p.h. and less in places, for the H.W.M. now had a very small safety margin and panic-braking was quite out of the question. This poor visibility continued for more than 15 miles and when it finally cleared the roads were in a very greasy condition. Conditions were not good and we had dropped more than 10 minutes behind our self-imposed schedule and, being unable to motor on full throttle, the engine started to fuss and one cylinder stopped working. This was getting depressing and just after Rovigo

the recent floods had washed about two miles of road completely away and a loose cart-track had been built to replace it. Over this the surface limited us to second gear and we took the opportunity of discussing the situation, deciding to continue to the first control at Ravenna, about 30 minutes farther on. Having dropped speed considerably we were re-passed by Meyer in his Aston Martin and we followed him down to Ferrara. It was now raining spasmodically and the roads were like sheets of ice at more than 100 m.p.h., and

in addition Abecassis had to cope with a car that was unstable at high speeds. Approaching a fairly sharp right-hand bend we were both suddenly aware that the Aston Martin in front of us was not going to get round it and, sure enough, the front wheels broke away and the car slid straight on. The next few seconds were very full for Tom Meyer while all we could do was to slow down and watch. The car ran along the left bank, bouncing so high that the sump was in full view, missed all the spectators and trees, slid back onto the road, spun gracefully round in front of us, struck a tree with its tail and fell on its side in the ditch at a very low speed. As we passed, the door opened and the passenger O'Hara climbed out and helped the driver out. Thinking very deep thoughts about tyre adhesion we continued on our way. Eventually we arrived at the control at Ravenna, had our card stamped and pulled over to our pre-arranged pit. The misfire proved to be something obscure in one of the Weber carburetters, while the damage at the rear was that the complete end of one of the telescopic shock-absorbers had broken off and was quite irreparable. As we were now 20 minutes behind schedule, with no hope of making up any time, only losing more, it was decided to retire, very reluctantly for the Mille Miglia only happens once a year and there really is nothing to equal it. A further trouble had become obvious in the last 20 miles into Ravenna and that was that the public were considering the race finished and were quite justifiably driving off home along the road on which we had been trying to race. We were the last starter and they had allowed us a certain measure of time and then considered the event finished. We had got behind this time allowance and it was going to be impossible to regain it. We had covered 200 miles and the race for us had hardly started; there was another 800 miles to cover, so we removed our crash-hats and went and had coffee. For the 200 miles from Brescia to Ravenna we had averaged 87 m.p.h. and that was too slow to justify continuing - a solemn thought indeed.

The adoption of the liberal Turismo Speciale regulations was one of the innovations of the XXI edition of the Mille Miglia. The usual Renault 4 CV 1063 equipped with a Claude 5-speed gearbox and driven by Jean Redelé and Louis Pons won the class at an average speed of over 105 kph but were beaten to the G. P. Nuvolari prize by their teammates J. Galtier and M. Michy (average speed 126.962 kph, photo 2).

1

The Fiat 1100/103 (3) of Ersilio Mandrini and Ferraris dominated the 1300 cc class with a average speed of over 110 kph, proving to be even faster on the Cremona-Brescia section. Piero Carini and Artesiani in turn dominated the over 1300 cc class with the Alfa Romeo 1900 TI (4) and also won the category overall in both the race and the Nuvolari GP (average speed 153.623 kph). They finished eighth overall at over 124 kph.

2

3

4

As was to be expected, the DB HBR (5) of Faure and Storez won the 750 cc Sport Internazionale class and also won the Nuvolari GP. The Porsche 550 (6) of Hans Herrmann and Herbert Linge won the 1500 cc class. The Italian flag was flown by the OSCA Mt4 2AD (7) of Giulio Cabianca who, in spite of giving away 400 cc to the Porsche, finished second in class, twenty minutes behind Herrmann, and won the 1500 Sport Internazionale class trophy on the Cremona-Brescia sectlegion at an average speed of over 162 kph.

In the Gran Turismo category victory in the 1500 cc class went to Richard Von Frankenberg and Sauter in the Porsche 1500 Super (1), whilst the 1300 cc sub-class was won by Hampel and Wolgang Von Trips in the Porsche 1300 Super (2). The over 1500 cc class and the category overall was won by Serafini and Mancini in a Lancia B 20 2500 GT (3) at an average speed of 124 kph. The respective classes in the Nuvolari GP were won by the same teams. Cipolla and Brioschi, on the other hand, won the Index of Performance with their Isetta (4).

The Autocar, 6 May 1955

MOSS GAINS HIS GREATEST VICTORY

First British Winner Shatters Mille Miglia Record in Mercedes: Fangio Second, Maglioli Third

In Italy last Saturday and Sunday Britain's Stirling Moss drove a Mercedes-Benz 300SLR to a brilliant victory in the Mille Miglia, the thousand miles race round a single lap of Italy through Brescia, Padua, Pescara, Rome, Bologna, Piacenza, Cremona and Mantua, back to Brescia. He was in complete command of the race most of the time, and in the process of winning shattered the existing record by some 10 m.p.h. He became the first British driver to win this classic event, and the first driver of any nationality to disprove the well-known maxim that the driver who leads at Rome will not win the race. His team-mate J. M. Fangio finished second, more than half an hour behind, and the Ferrari of Maglioli was third. Only one British car was regarded as being seriously in the running for the major award - the DB3S Aston Martin works entry - and this car, driven by Peter Collins, had to retire soon after the half-way mark. Austin-Healeys, having an engine size of more than 2 litres, had to compete with the most powerful cars, and the Triumph TR2s were up against Maseratis and Ferraris in the 2-litre class. Imagine having an early breakfast and leaving London by car at

about 7.15 a.m., reaching Aberdeen by lunch-time, and getting back to London in time for a latish tea - with only two stops. That, on roads that are admittedly better than British roads, parallels the achievement of Stirling Moss last weekend in winning the 22nd Mille Miglia. Sometimes his car was reaching nearly 170 m.p.h. on the

straight, but often the roads are narrow and lined with concrete posts.

The race took place in blazing sunshine. Moss' companion was bearded Dennis Jenkinson, well known in another sphere as an ace sidecar rider.

The Mille Miglia, through the years, has gained rather than lost in stature, for the organiza-

tion is unusually quick to seize upon any form of improvement. This time, for example, there was a special prize for the best sports car costing not more than two million lire in Italy, a class from which the very expensive Ferraris and their brethren were automatically excluded. And there was a special section from Cremona to Mantua for which there was a speed prize in honour of the great Tazio Nuvolari, who was born in Mantua.

ON THE PAVEMENTS....

Brescia is one of those towns that earns the title of quaint the hard way: in many streets the pavements are on the same level as the roadway, so that the local drivers inevitably spend as much time on the pavements as in the narrow roads. Its squares are impressive, and the race visitor gets the immediate impression that the town is alive.

Hot sunshine beat down on to the Piazza Vittoria for several days before the race, and as each day went by the big crowds that assembled early in the morning swelled until by late afternoon the whole square was

The poster for the twenty-second edition of the Mille Miglia dominated by Moss and Jenkinson in the Mercedes 300 SLR.

1

Two views of the scrutineering in Piazza della Vittoria. In photo 1, the officials are examining the Maserati A6GCSs. In the foreground is the car of the Tuscan driver Siro Sbraci (no. 631) who finished 12th overall. A photo from the "Mille Miglia Tower" (2). From left to right and from bottom to top can be recognised the Ermini 1100 of Fontana (no. 530), the OSCA Mt4 2AD of Claude Bourillot (no. 518), the Moretti 750 designed by Giovanni Michelotti of the Italfrance team driven by L. Renault (no. 005), the Fiat 8V of P. Bianchedi (no. 632), the Italfrance team's Moretti 750 driven by Lino Fayen (no. 043), the DB HBR of J. Pages (no. 028), the Zagato 750 MM of Messedaglia (no. 033), the Maserati A6GCS of Lopez (no. 625), the Lancia Aurelia Zagato of Ferdinando Gutta (no. 654), the A6GCS of Palmer Aprile (no. 640) and the Branca Moretti of Aquilino Branca (no. 040).

packed with excited Italians, all hoping to catch a glimpse of the cars and the favourite drivers. The cars were driven, or in some cases carried on trailers, to one side of the square where the scrutineering bay was roped off from the crowds. After examination they would pass through the eager spectators to get away, so that no matter where a spectator might be in the throng he was likely to see something of the competing machines.

They were all immaculately turned out. On the day before the race the morning scrutineering saw a shining column of Austin-Healeys, with Donald Healey (standing by to settle queries) shooting away with a camera as enthusiastically as the spectators. At the same time two of the formidable 300SLR Mercedes stood by on trailers awaiting their turn.

Later, the loudspeakers announced that Fangio had arrived to see his car through, and at once people started to run from all sides of the piazza to get a

2

glimpse of the world champion, cheering and waving as they went. A little later the performance was repeated to mark the arrival of Moss. With an entry of 648 cars, of which 533 started, scrutineering took days, of course, and the excitement continued to grow all the time. Slowly information began to leak out about the cars that really mattered - the big sports cars that would cover the 1,000 miles at the highest speeds. Before the race began there was no mistaking the favourites - Mercedes-Benz. The 300SLR cars had not been seen before, but it was soon confirmed that they differed only in minor respects from the successful Grand Prix cars. Their engine size had been increased to 3 litres (2,980 c.c.).

When the G.P. car was introduced last year it was clear that there would be no difficulty in adding a passenger's seat, and so the SLR body looks little different from that of the racing car. The engine is a straight eight

The Mercedes Benz works team heads for scrutineering in Piazza della Vittoria.

with exactly "square" bore and stroke. It has fuel injection, dual ignition, dry sump lubrication, and the valves are closed mechanically. The car has a five-speed gear box, with synchromesh on second to fifth gears. Suspension is by torsion bars, with swing axles at the rear. Power output and possible maximum speeds were kept secret at Brescia, but it was believed that in the race the speeds on the autostrada would be at least 170 m.p.h.

But Mercedes were not favourites merely because the cars seemed so formidable. The drivers included Fangio, Moss, Kling and Hermann, all of whom had been practising hard. British hopes for an outright win were slender, being pinned to the lone DB3S Aston Martin of Peter Collins. There were two other Aston entries, but these were saloons in another class. Britain was well represented in the 2-litres sports car class by the Triumph TR2s of Scott-Russel and Haig, Steed and Bruce,

and Brooke and Fairman, but they were up against swarms of Ferraris and Maseratis. The Austin-Healeys, having an engine size of over 2,000 c.c., were in the unlimited class, obviously with little chance of an outright win. However, this year the new special prize had been introduced, and the Austin-Healeys had a very good chance of winning it. The prize served to emphasize the very great price difference that exists between most British sports cars and such famous Italian makes as Ferrari.

But if British hopes were almost non-existent, so were those of most other countries. Before the race it was thought that the Maseratis would be virtually the

G.P. cars with an extra seat and appropriate modifications. Also, most Italian drivers know the course. Those who live in Rome and make fairly regular journeys to Milan, for example, can not only follow the second half of the course one way and the first half going home but can concentrate on learning the road by such frequent trips. Of the Mercedes drivers, only Kling had really wide experience of the route, having covered a total of fifty laps (about 50,000 miles).

Unfortunately, only one 3-litre Maserati made an appearance, in the hands of Valenzano and Perdisa, and it did not meet with success. Ferraris entered their 3-litre cars, but these were not new, and they were not consid-

ered real contenders for the major award.

ENTHUSIASM, KNOWLEDGE

The fascination of this principal Italian sports car race has several sources, not the least of which is the enthusiasm and extraordinary motoring knowledge of the people of the country. Throughout the race every Italian-owned television set and radio is tuned to the event, and the latest news of the leading cars is exchanged in the street between strangers, excitedly passed on to customers by restaurant waiters, and vigorously debated in almost every public place. The first car was flagged away at 9 p.m. from a tree-lined avenue in Brescia in which the crowds would remain to see the cars return to base. The air was noisy with the imploring advertising announcements, the babble of the stallholders, the fuss of the soldiery, the fire brigade…

In the avenue is a ramp from which the cars start, quickly

switching from side to head lamps as they plunge into the darkness a hundred yards ahead. Throughout the night the ramp is floodlit, and the constant crowd can be relied upon to produce as fitting a cheer for a 2 c.v. Citroen as for the great contenders for victory.

Although the first cars were under way just after 9 p.m., it was morning before, at one-minute intervals, the big cars set off to overhaul them. The most important category was that for sports cars of over 2-litres capacity, and dawn had broken before they left. J. M. Fangio was one of the early starters in this class, and following him one minute later was the Austin-Healey of G. Abecassis. Soon they were all on the road, and the real struggle began. Along the route the crowds were gathered in little

knots, huddled together against the chill morn breeze. There are a number of tricky right- and left-hand bends between Brescia and Vicenza, and at each of these local people had gathered to peer excitedly up the road as the scream of an exhaust came over on the morning air. In the early hours the Fiat 1100 cars passed, swinging up clouds of dust, but going most impressively and holding the road splendidly. At dawn the field had still not grown in engine size beyond the 1,100 c.c. sports stage, but there was the promise of more exciting machinery to come and the tiny villages were thronged. Cortese's Fiat 8V was going very fast, and soon afterwards came the bigger cars, Ferraris and Mercedes. Moss arrived at a tricky left-hander on the tail of a Ferrari and took the corner visibly faster

than any other competitor, even including Fangio, stilling the crowd to momentary silence before excitement broke out again as the Mercedes went on to overtake the Ferrari in the next bend. Time passed and reports filtered in from the farther districts; the order began to settle down. At Ravenna, Galtier's Renault led its class and Fiats completely dominated theirs led by Morolli. Bayol led the 750 c.c. sports class in his D.B., and the American John Fitch the unlimited Gran Turismo class in a 300SL Mercedes. He was followed by two similar cars and da Silva's Aston Martin.

Among the fastest cars Moss was soon in the lead. At Ancona Taruffi was but 34sec behind in a Ferrari which had started last. Then came the Mercedes 300SLR of Hans Herrmann,

Castellotti's Ferrari, Karl Kling's Mercedes, Maglioli's Ferrari, and Fangio's Mercedes.

Moss made only two stops for fuel (including changing the wheels at the second one, in Rome). He could not, of course, know how close Taruffi might be on his tail, but Italian hopes were dashed when the Ferrari lost its oil pressure and had to retire. So mile after mile the leading silver car kept hurtling on.

Mercedes were also sweeping the field in the unlimited Gran Turismo class. At Pescara John Fitch had established a lead in the 300SL over the similar cars of Gendebien and Casella, with da Silva's Aston fourth. Herrmann distinguished himself by holding third and fourth places successively for a long time in the general classification, but he was particularly unlucky in being put out of the race by a stone that made a hole in the Mercedes' fuel tank after Rome. Fangio, in eighth place at Ravenna, steadily caught up several of those in front of him, and at Pescara was

Again the Thirion-Washer team, this time during the race near San Benedetto del Tronto with what was described after the race as a "Porsche tipo 550". The pair finished 57th overall and sixth in the 1100-1500 cc Sport Internazionale class.

fifth behind Kling. It seemed that his car was running well but not with full power. However, he continued to move up, partly owing to the mortality rate of the cars in front.

LOCAL IMPRESSION

At Rome the race had lost Castellotti's Ferrari, leaving only Taruffi to challenge Moss seriously; Herrmann was third and Fangio fourth. The drama of Moss' passage through the age-old city could be no better conveyed than by this impression from an English resident:

"It was a proud moment to see Stirling roar down the Via Salaria into Rome, leading Taruffi by two minutes....

"When we arrived on the course 12 kilometres outside the city at half-past seven we realized that Moss had left Brescia at 7.22 a.m., over 500 miles away and one of the last cars to depart (a great help to spectators is the fact that the cars bear the number corresponding to their starting time). So it seemed incredible

that five hours and one minute later we saw him flash past, leading the Mercedes team by minutes.

"On our left sat an excited Italian with a portable radio which, at around eleven o'clock, had announced that Taruffi was just ahead of the field at Pescara, having averaged the incredible speed of 117.44 m.p.h. He had left Brescia six minutes after Moss. The excitement in the large Italian crowd was enormous. Every red Alfa Romeo or Maserati was hailed as the red Ferrari. However, the minutes passed and then at last Taruffi appeared - but eight minutes after Moss. "The cry immediately went up that the first driver into Rome had never won the Mille Miglia; but we kept our fingers crossed. The crowd departed and we were left waiting for the news from Brescia.

"Poor Taruffi. Magnificent Moss!" Soon they were over the Futa Pass (where Herrmann dropped out) and heading for home. At Cremona the smaller cars were

already racing through the streets, and starting the 60-kilometre timed section to Mantua for the Nuvolari prize. On the Sunday afternoon the cars began to finish their marathon. There were gaps in the ranks, and many cars were battered. Among the British drivers missing was Flockhart, who had crashed but had been thrown clear into a river, to suffer only from a cold! Austin-Healeys were upholding British prestige, so far as they were able in the unlimited class. Until quite late in the race, the car driven by George Abecassis was well up towards the front, but towards the end the very fast, big cars began to overtake him one by one. Even so, he finished eleventh in the general classification and all through the long hours of passage was averaging more than 80 m.p.h. The honour of being the first British car home was to fall to this Austin-Healey, and it was also to be fifth in its class - for sports cars over 2 litres.

Lance Macklin's car, too, added

lustre to the reputation of the make, keeping up an average of nearly 80 m.p.h. When at last he was to cross the finishing line his car would be eighth in the class, and Donald Healey would have good reason to click the shutter again.

The sun still blazed, and the crowds in the finishing line waited for Moss, whose progress was reported over the loudspeakers every few minutes: "Moss is in Cremona... Moss is in Mantua... Moss is in Montechiari..."

Then suddenly the bedlam of the exhaust was mingling with the swelling volume of cheers and a British driver, even if in a German car, hurtled over the line first, and for the first time, in one of the world's great and classic races, a race in which the non-Italian must drive against an almost insuperable handicap.

Passenger Jenkinson, one great, beaming smile under his crash helmet, waved both hands in the air. The crowds responded with a thousand programmes. The 1955 Mille Miglia had been won. Myths had been exploded, records shattered. For once, and deservedly, fortune had smiled on Stirling Moss.

Motor Sport, June, 1955

XXII 1000 MIGLIA

Stirling Moss Makes History with a Decisive Win for Mercedes-Benz

Brescia, May 1st.

The fabulous Italian sports-car race, the Mille Miglia, took place over the week-end of April 30th-May 1st, but preparations for the event began many months before, not only amongst the big firms whose aim was an outright win, but also amongst all the various classes for the XXII Mille Miglia contained 14 different classes, from diesel-engined cars and touring cars, through Gran Turismo groups to free-for-all sports categories, permitting thinly-disguised Grand Prix cars. Naturally, the main force for the outright winner comes from the Sports Class over 2,000 c.c., and Mercédès-Benz were testing their new 300SLR model in Italy as early as February, having already used the engine in their Formule Libre Grand Prix cars in the Argentine. The Ferrari factory had also used the Argentine races to try out their new six-cylinder 3,750-c.c. sports car and also had a re-sounding victory with it in the Tour of Sicily. Maserati raced their new 3-litre six-cylinder model, derived very directly from the For-mula I car, in Sebring, Sicily and Dakar. These three firms were the main protagonists for the XXII

Mille Miglia, and as the end of April approached activity around Italy became much more notice-able.

Italian drivers enter the Mille Miglia as a sort of tradition and they filled all the classes with every type of vehicle imaginable, and with an enormous German entry of diesel, 300SL, and the factory team of 300 SLR Mer-cédès-Benz, Porsches, both standard and sports, together with a very large British entry, most of it of a sporting rather than serious nature, and numer-ous French cars in the smaller-engine capacity classes, a total of 652 entries were received. Not all of these presented themselves for the scrutineering and many of those that did had little intention of going very far round the

course, but the tradition of the Mille Miglia is such that enthusi-asts in and around Brescia are happy to enter and retire a few kilometres up the road, just to swell the numbers and enjoy the wonderful atmosphere of the start. Altogether 521 cars started in the race, leaving at one-minute intervals from the main road to the east out of Brescia, each car's number being its actual starting time.

Scrutineering took place in the main square of Brescia during the three days before the race, and on Friday Mercédès-Benz took their four 300SLR model along, two at a time, on an enor-mous trailer. The first pair were those of Fangio and Kling, both of them driving alone, with the passenger seat covered over

and a Perspex screen enveloping the driver on both sides, with a single headrest behind the driver. The second pair were those of Moss and Herrmann, they both taking passengers with them, the former with the MOTOR SPORT Continental Correspondent, Jenkinson, and the latter with a Mercédès-Benz mechanic, Her-man Eger. These cars had two long headrests forming part of the tail and looked particularly fierce sports cars, the other two looking more like Grand Prix cars. Mechanically all four were identi-cal, using the same layout of me-chanical detail as the W196 Grand Prix Mercédès-Benz, with the near-horizontal eight-cylinder fuel-injection, desmodromic valve engine, five-speed gearbox on the rear axle, torsion-bar and wishbone i.f.s., and torsion-bar swing-axle rear suspension; all brakes were mounted inboard, steering was left-hand, and two short stub pipes protruded from the side of the car just in front of the passenger seat. The 3-litre engines were developing 295 b.h.p. at 7,500 r.p.m., the fuel tank in the tail held 260 litres, and they were anticipating making only two stops, one at Pescara for a small quantity of fuel and the other at Rome for rear tyres and

Stirling Moss and Denis Jenkinson in close-up and on the ramp prior to the start (below).

to fill the tank right up.
The whole Mercédès-Benz approach to the Mille Miglia was one of thoroughness, all the cars carrying two spare wheels in the tail, one front and one rear, while quickly attachable aluminium aero-screens could be fitted in front of the permanent Perspex

screen should it become smashed by a stone or a bird. The afternoon saw the square crowded with spectators from almost all countries, there being large contingents of English and American visitors, and almost until dark the four scrutineers bays dealt with competitors' cars,

making sure the standard cars were standard, especially the Gran Turismo categories, and wiring a circular fibre disc to the steering column of all cars. These discs had to be punched at the Rome and Bologna controls, in addition to the route card handed over at the start, which

had to be stamped at the controls at Ravenna, Pescara, Aquila, Rome, Siena, Firenze, Bologna and Mantova.
On Saturday morning a swarm of 2-litre Maseratis arrived driven by works driver Musso down to comparative newcomers, and also in this class were five TR2 Triumphs, Scott-Russell, Steed and Brooke on English ones and a French one and a Swiss one. In the over-2,000-c.c. class only one 3-litre Maserati was presented, to be driven by the new young Italian driver Perdisa. There were many 3-litre four-cylinder Ferraris, privately owned, but it was not until nearly lunch-time that the works Ferraris drove in, amidst wild cheering and booming exhaust notes. Until now the programme had contained a long row of Xs beside the Ferrari numbers, and speculation had been high as to who was to drive them. Maglioli, Sighinolfi, Carini, Paolo Marzotto and Taruffi were all on the new 3,750-c.c. six-cylinder models, with de Dion rear ends and five-speed gearboxes, while Castellotti was on loan from Lancia and had been given a 4.4-litre six-cylinder Ferrari.
Starting positions in the Mille Miglia are arranged by ballot and

Juan Manuel Fangio was well beaten by Stirling Moss, finishing half an hour down on the Englishman at the Brescia finish.

it was now clear as to the form the race would take. Mercédès-Benz drivers were Fangio 658, Kling 701 and Herrmann 704, and the X on 705 had been given to Maglioli; Carini was 714, on his own amongst a number of private owners. Moss was 722, and the numbers 723, 724, 725 were works Ferraris, as was 728. The Maranello firm arranged their drivers in the order Castellotti, Sighinolfi, Marzotto and Taruffi, so that the young Britisher had a formidable array behind him, added to which 726 was Bordoni with a 3-litre Gordini, and 727 was Perdisa. Also in this class was a lone Aston Martin DB3S, driven by Collins, 702, and Austin-Healeys driven by Abecassis, Flockhart, Macklin, Healey and an Italian named Verilli, but they could not hope to cause any bother to the might of Stuttgart and Maranello. The whole of the scrutineering was carried out under a hot sun shining from a cloudless sky and it seemed certain that race day would prove fine, and it was expected that records would be broken.

At 9 p.m. on Saturday night the diesel class of Mercédès-Benz and Fiat cars began to leave, and they were followed by a bunch of 250-c.c. Isettas, a row of 2 c.v. Citroëns, some of them very highly tuned, and even with lowered bodywork, for all this was

the Series Special Class in which modifications were allowed. Leaving at minute intervals, this group seemed to go on for ever, with Fiat 500, Fiat 600, Renault and Panhard entries. Following these went an enormous class reserved solely for absolutely standard 1,100 Fiat and Lancia Appia cars, and just after midnight the first of the 750-c.c. sports cars left. The volume of noise increased as Siata, Moretti, Stanguellini, Fiat, Giannini, Bandini and various "one-off" cars joined the fray to do battle with Panhard, D.B. and Renault sports models in a very serious Franco/Italian duel. The touring class up to 1,300 c.c. was a long row of "Millecento" Fiats, livened up a bit by some D.K.W.s and Peugeots and a lonely Volkswagen. Special Fiats dominated the Gran Turismo class up to 1,100 c.c., and then came a most interesting group. This was the Gran Turismo up to 1,300 c.c., and more than 30 Alfa-Romeo Giulietta Sprints were making their first Mille Miglia ap-

pearance. Interspersed among the Italian cars were nine 1,300-c.c. Porsche Super models. This class was to be followed closely by all Italians and Germans, as well as many others. The over-1,300-c.c. touring class consisted mostly of 1,900 Alfa-Romeo models, but not so many as in previous years, no doubt many drivers changing to the smaller Giulietta models.

At 3.52 a.m. on Sunday morning the really fast cars began to leave in the over-1,300-c.c. Gran Turismo group, and this contained Porsche 1,500 Super, Lancia Aurelia, Mercédès-Benz 300 SL, Alfa-Romeo Sprint, Fiat 8V, a lone Jaguar 140 coupé, a 203 Salmson and two works Aston Martin DB2/4. The numerous Porsches were obviously badly handicapped by having to go in this class against much bigger cars, and hot favourites were the 300SL models, while the Aston Martins could not be ignored, being driven by Paul Frere and Wisdom. The Mercédès-Benz were in the hands of Fitch, Gendebien,

Peters and Casella, and as all cars had to be strictly to catalogue the performances in this class held everyone's attention. It was still dark as an almost all-Italian class of 1,100-c.c. sports cars set off, comprised of numerous Fiat Specials, Osca and Stanguellini entries, and they were followed by the 1,500-c.c. sports class. This category should have seen the first appearance of the new 1,500-c.c. Maserati, but none was ready in time. However, four Porsche 550 Spiders opposed three Oscas, three Siatas, two special Giuliettas, a Peugeot, an Ermini and a lone Gordini, the last driven by the two Belgian girls, Thirion and Washer. At eight minutes past 6 a.m. the row of TR2 Triumphs began to leave, followed by a multitude of 2-litre Maseratis and three Mondial Ferraris, Taramazzo and Leto di Priolo driving factory cars and Cornacchia a very similar model.

By now it was broad daylight and the real giants of the race were lined up behind the starting ramp awaiting their time to be off on the 1,000 miles of normal Italian roads, passing through villages, towns and cities, along dead-straight coastal roads and crossing mountain passes, every imaginable type of road being covered by the route, which must

surely constitute the toughest racing circuit in the world on which to drive a near-Grand Prix car. The noise of the Mercédès-Benz and Ferrari cars was accentuated by the silence of the Austin-Healeys, and as Taruffi drove down the starting ramp at 7.28 a.m. the cheering and waving reached a climax, and the 1955 Mille Miglia was completely under way. By now, of course, many of the cars were well on their way round the 1,000 miles, and, equally, many had retired or crashed, for the accident rate in

this race is high, though injuries surprisingly small.

As was expected, Castellotti set the pace, his 4.4-litre proving too fast for the Mercédès-Benz, and at Ravenna he was leading Moss by nearly 2 min., and behind came Taruffi, Herrmann, Kling, Maglioli, Perdisa and Fangio, the Argentinian not really feeling in the true Mille Miglia spirit. Marzotto had retired just after Verona when a tyre burst at over 160 m.p.h., the ensuing dice frightening him sufficiently for him not to want to risk another. Castellotti was going

all out to try and break up the German cars, but he too had tyre trouble and then between Ravenna and Pescara the Ferrari engine could not stand the pace and blew up. By now Moss had taken the lead, but after they had all clocked in at Pescara Taruffi had got in front by 15 sec., and Moss was followed by Herrmann, Kling, Fangio and Maglioli, the rest being far behind. Everyone was driving to the limit of their cars and the average at Ravenna had been 192.414 k.p.h., while, after passing through the hills behind Ancona and the numerous villages down the Adriatic coast, Taruffi had averaged 189.909 k.p.h., all records being surpassed by a margin undreamed of by even the most optimistic follower. At Pescara Mercédès-Benz and Ferrari had refuelling stations and, while Moss stopped for only 28 sec., Taruffi was stationary for more than 60 sec. and set off again, now no longer in the lead, amid hoots and whistles from the crowd. Moss still led at the Aquila control, but Taruffi was ever present

in second place, followed by Herrmann, Kling and Fangio. With Castellotti and Marzotto out of the race and Maglioli still suffering from a damaged arm incurred during practice, the Ferrari hopes looked forlorn, especially as Carini and Sighinolfi just could not cope with the pace. The lone Maserati of Perdisa was running in seventh place but too far behind to count. At Rome, after crossing the mountains through Antrodoco and down to Rieti, Moss had gained an advantage of nearly 2 min., but still Taruffi clung on, driving desperately, but his task looked hopeless as he was followed by Herrmann, Kling and Fangio, and all four Mercédès-Benz cars seemed set to finish the course.

On the first bend after the Rome hairpin Kling slid off the road and smashed his car against the trees, wrecking it completely, but fortunately with no very severe damage to himself, and not long after this Taruffi ran into trouble, and he arrived at the main Ferrari depot at Viterbo with an oil pump having failed. The Mercédès-

The Triumph TR2 of the Belgian Marguiraz and Huguenin at the start.

Benz team had refuelled and changed rear tyres at Rome and intended to go through non-stop to Brescia, but the pace was telling, for Moss had averaged 173.021 k.p.h. to Rome, and after Taruffi's trouble Fangio had one of the injection pipes split and ran on seven cylinders most of the way to Firenze, the next Mercédès-Benz depot. This allowed Perdisa to make up lost ground, and though Mercédès-Benz were 1-2-3 at Firenze the Maserati was not far behind the third German car. The only Ferrari left in the running was Maglioli, but, in addition to suffering with his damaged arm, his car's shock-absorbers had given out and then a petrol pipe broke, so that he dropped a long way back. Moss was really out to win now and he never let up at all, his average at Firenze being 157.064 k.p.h., and he set out over the Futa and Raticosa passes with renewed vigour, there being no one to approach his performance.

At the top of the Futa Herrmann had trouble with his fuel tank filler and had to retire as it was impossible to corner without being soaked in petrol, and also on this section Perdisa's Maserati broke down with engine trouble, so that Moss was now out on his own, leading the race at Bologna by nearly 28 min. from Fangio, but still the British team in the German car did not let up and over the final stretch from Cremona to Brescia Moss averaged 198.496 k.p.h., an enormous speed when it is remembered that this included stopping at Mantova to have the route card stamped. His overall average for the race was 157.650 k.p.h., beating the old record of Giannino Marzotto by over 15 k.p.h., and he covered the 1,000 miles in 10 hr. 07 min. 48 sec. After the Firenze control Fangio's Mercédès-Benz went properly again, but he could not catch the flying Moss and he finished second, while behind him struggled Maglioli. The rest of the over-2,000-c.c.

sports cars that finished were so slow that 2-litre and Gran Turismo cars filled the next seventh places.

Of the various class battles the 1,300 Porsches completely trounced all the Alfa-Romeo Giuliettas, the Mercédès-Benz 300SL cars dominated their class from start to finish, Maserati

Sports, 750 c.c.:

1st: Storez (D.B. Panhard) 13 hr. 21 min. 03 sec. - 119.618
2nd: Auricchio (Stanguellini) 13 hr. 55 min. 22 sec.
3rd: Navarro (Panhard) 13 hr. 58 min. 01 sec.

Special Series Touring 1,300 c.c.:

1st: Mandrini / Berton (Fiat 1,100-c.c.)
      13 hr. 48 min. 12 sec. - 115.697
2nd: Villotti (Fiat 1,100-c.c.) 13 hr. 58 min. 12 sec.
3rd: Guiraud / Abaud (Peugeot 203) 14 hr. 09 min. 04 sec.

Gran Turismo, 1,100 c.c.:

1st: Viola (Fiat 1,100-c.c.) 14 hr. 32 min. 50 sec. - 109.780
2nd: Tiozzo / Poggi (Fiat 1,100-c.c.) 14 hr. 54 min. 27 sec.
3rd: Kerschbaumer/Peristi (Fiat 1,100-c.c.) 15 hr. 38 min. 40 sec.

Gran Turismo, 1,300 c.c.:

1st: v. Frankenberg / Oberndorff (Porsche)
      12 hr. 58 min. 39 sec. - 123.059
2nd: v. Trips (Porsche) 13 hr. 02 min. 55 sec.
3rd: Buticchi (Alfa-Romeo) 13 hr. 17 min. 18 sec.

Special Series Touring, over 1,300 c.c.:

1st: Cestelli / Musso (Alfa-Romeo 1,900)
      13 hr. 14 min. 05 sec. - 120.667
2nd: Sala / Vigliani (Alfa-Romeo 1,900) 13 hr. 14 min. 57 sec.
3rd: Stern / Barbery (Alfa-Romeo 1,900)
      13 hr. 15 min. 51 sec.

Gran Turismo, over 1,300 c.c.:

1st: Fitch / Gessl (Mercédès-Benz 300SL)
      11 hr. 29 min. 21 sec. - 139.000
2nd: Gendebien / Washer (Mercédès-Benz SL)
      11 hr. 36 min. 00 sec.
3rd: Casella (Mercédès-Benz 300SL) 12 hr. 11 min. 15 sec.

Sports, 1,100 c.c.:

1st: Bourillot (Osca) 13 hr. 01 min. 21 sec. - 122.634
2nd: Colantoni / Foglia (Osca) 13 hr. 12 min. 27 sec.
3rd: Nobile / Bettiol (Osca) 13 hr. 18 min. 38 sec.

Sports, 1,500 c.c.:

1st: Seidel / Glockler (Porsche 550)
      12 hr. 08 min. 17 sec. - 131.570
2nd: Descollanges / Nicol (Osca) 12 hr. 29 min. 56 sec.
3rd: Lautenschlager / Scholl (Porsche 550)
      12 hr. 59 min. 52 sec.

Sports, 2,000 c.c.:

1st: Giardini (Maserati A6G) 11 hr. 15 min. 32 sec. - 141.843
2nd: Bellucci (Maserati A6G) 12 hr. 09 min. 10 sec.
3rd: Sbraci (Maserati A6G) 12 hr. 24 min. 31 sec.

Sports, over 2,000 c.c.:

1st: Moss / Jenkinson (Mercédès-Benz 300SLR)
      10 hr. 07 min. 48 sec. - 157.650
2nd: Fangio (Mercédès-Benz 300SLR) 10 hr. 39 min. 33 sec.
3rd: Maglioli / Monteferrario (Ferrari 3.7)
      10 hr. 52 min. 47 sec.

Total starters: 521. Total finishers: 281.

G. P. of Nuvolari (fastest time Cremona-Mantova-Brescia - 134 kilometres)

S. Moss / D. Jenkinson (Mercédès-Benz), 39 min. 54 sec. - 198.496 k.p.h.

---

won the 2-litre sports class, and Seidel and Glockler brought their 550 Porsche home first in the 1,550-c.c. class, but only after Cabianca's Osca broke down in the mountains after Firenze.

MILLE MIGLIA MUSINGS

Moss drove as hard as possible for the whole 1,600 kilometres and was not aware Taruffi had retired until he reached Brescia.

* * *

Gendebien had the bad luck to puncture a tyre just before arriving at Brescia, while leading his class; this delay let Fitch into the lead. The Belgian driver arrived at the Mille Miglia just having recovered from an illness and only saw his SL two days before the race.

* * *

The Aston Martin DB3S of Peter Collins was fitted with disc brakes, and these necessitated of peculiar wire-spoked wheels with very offset rims, in order to clear the brakes pads and keep the centre line of the tyre in the right place. Some Lancia Aurelias were also fitted with this type of wire wheel.

* * *

The lone VW in the touring class looped the loop soon after the start, but the American driver Newcombe was unhurt. Equally, Millecento Fiats, Giuliettas, Aurelias and Ferraris all wrote themselves off. To crash in the Mille Miglia is no disgrace.

* * *

The two Aston Martin DB2/4 models were the factory ones used in the Monte Carlo Rally.

Neither of them finished the Mille Miglia, though they got a bit farther than the DB3S.

* * *

J.B. (H.W.M.) Heath had a comfortable ride round on his own in a Jaguar 140 coupé, his first Mille Miglia, and he finished 40th.

* * *

The efforts of Abecassis in the Austin-Healey were very good, finishing ahead of many 2-litre Maseratis. Lance Macklin also completed the course, but Flockhart finished up in a ditch and

Left, the arrive of M. Cipolla with his Isotta at Brescia.
Bottom, the Austin Healey 100 S of Donald Healey and Cashmore (on the left) and the Triumph TR2 of Brooke and Lampe (59th overall).

Healey stopped for breakfast after all the fast cars had overtaken him, for the roads then became open.

* * *

The Belgian girl Gilberte Thirion completed the course in a works 1,500-c.c. Gordini, finishing 57th, but she lost a lot of time due to running out of petrol.

* * *

The Porsche driver Trips was leading his class when the throttle linkage broke. He wired the butterfly fully open and drove on the ignition switch for the last quarter of the race, and this dropped him to second place in his class.

* * *

Bayol broke the rear suspension of his D.B. Panhard and the wheels leant against the body, but being f.w.d. he was able to make the car drag itself back to the finish.

* * *

The astounding 250-c.c. Iso-Isettas, the things that are the same measurements no matter from which angle they are viewed, with four little wheelbarrow wheels, averaged 50 m.p.h. to Rome.

* * *

There were at least eight 300SL Mercédès-Benz in Brescia during race week, and more Porsches than one cares to imagine.

Stirling Moss and Denis Jenkinson with their Mercedes 300 SLR (1) not only won at the record average speed of 157.650 kph, but also conquered the Index of Performance and the Nuvolari GP at an average speed of over 198 kph. They preceded over the finishing line the Mercedes 300 SLR of Juan Manuel Fangio (2), the Ferrari 118 LM (3) of Maglioli an Monteferrario, the Maserati A6GCS of Francesco Giardini (1st in the 2000 cc SI class, photo 4) and the Mercedes 300 SI of Fitch and Kurt (1st in the over 1300 cc GT class and category winners of the Nuvolari GP, photo 5).

The 1100 and 1300 cc GT classes were won respectively by the Fiat 1100 TV Pininfarina of F. Viola (photo 1) and the Porsche 1300 Super of Von Frankenberg and Oberndorff (2) who also won the Nuvolari GP for the class. The up to 1600 cc sub-class was won by the Porsche 1500 Super of R. Günzler (3) and the up to 2000 cc sub-class by the Fiat 8V Zagato of the Leto di Priolo brothers (4).

1

3

4

2

The DB HBR (1) of Claude Storez
won the 750 cc class of the Sport Internazionale category as well as the
relative Nuvolari GP, as did the OS-
CA Mt4 2AD (2) of Claude Bourillot
and the Porsche 550 of Wolfgang
Seidel and Helm Glöckler (3). The
special class reserved for open cars
was won by the Austin Healey 100 S
(4) driven by George Abbecassis.

In the myriad classes and sub-classes into which the Turismo category was divided, the Mercedes 180 D (1) of Retter and Larcher won the group reserved for diesel cars, the Alpine Renault (3) of Galtier and Michy the 750 Turismo Speciale group and the Nuvolari GP. The Fiat 1100/103 TV (2) driven by Mandrini - Bertossi won the 1300 cc Turismo Speciale class whilst the example driven by Rabuffi and Lenti was fastest over the Cremona-Brescia section. Victory in the category went to the Alfa Romeo 1900 TI (4) of Cestelli Guidi and Giuseppe Musso at an average speed of over 124 kph.

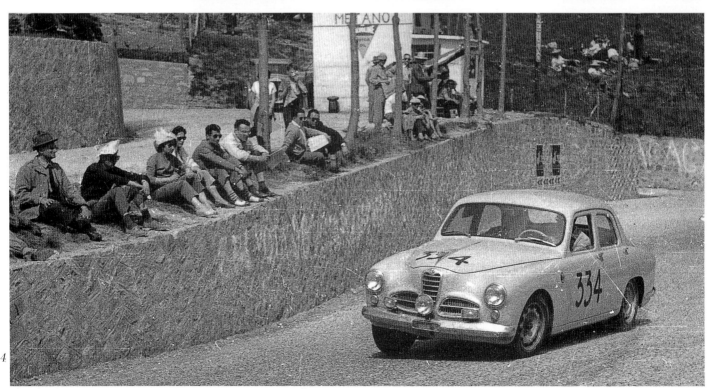

In the sub-classes of the Turismo Speciale category victory went to the Citroen 2 CV (5) of G. Seibert in the 500 cc division, to Omati-Corazza (6) in the Fiat 500 sub-class, to Soldaini-Giannotti among the Fiat 600s and to the DKW Sonder-klasse (7) of Spiliotakis-Spiliotakis in the 1000 cc division.

5

6

7

The Peugeot 203 Darl'mat (8) of Guiraud About won the 1151-1300 sub-class of the Turismo Speciale category, whilst the sub-class reserved for Fiat 1100s and Lancia Appias in the Turismo Normale category saw victory go to the Fiat of Olinto Morolli overall, and to the example driven by Gino de Sanctis in the Nuvolari G.P. at an average speed of 133.859 km/h.

8

Cagli and Banti with their Borgward Isabella (2) won the up to 1600 cc sub-class of the Turismo Speciale category, whilst the Mercedes 220 (1) of Zedlitz and Diemer won the over 2000 cc sub-class. The special class for sports cars derived from touring and GT cars saw victory go to the Fiat 8V Zagato (3) of Franco Cortese and Stazzi, whilst the Alfa Romeo 1900 TI (4) of Stern and Barbery won the Nuvolari GP for the Turismo Speciale category at an average speed of over 149 kph.

1

2

3

4

A THOUSAND WET MILES

Resounding Ferrari victory in the Mille Miglia

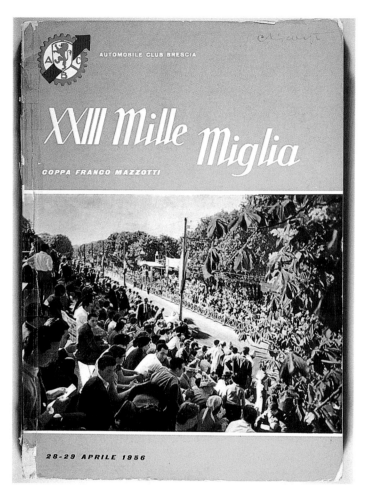

In appalling weather conditions of torrential rain and of fog on high ground, Eugenio Castellotti's 12-cylinder, 3 1/2 litre Ferrari won last weekend's Mille Miglia at a speed of 84,9 m.p.h. Following him across the line came four more Ferraris-Peter Collins, Luigi Musso, Manuel Fangio and Oliver Gendebien. Last year's winner, Stirling Moss, whose Maserati was not ready until the day of the race, retired at half-distance.

Though unplaced in the general classification, British cars featured in the class results. In the up to 2-litre class for sports cars with a basic price limit of 2,000,000 lire, M.G. As came second, third and fifth, with a Triumph TR2 in fourth position. In the over 2-litre section of the same class, a Jaguar won, with an Austin-Healey second. In the 1,100-1,500 c.c. sports car class M.G. As were fourth, fifth and sixth, beaten only by such potent and expensive opposition as Osca, Maserati and Porsche. Finally, in the 1,300-1,600 c.c. section of the special series production class, two Sunbeam Rapiers, on their first international race, came second and third. The drivers of open cars had a formidable task to keep going in the weather conditions that last-

ed throughout the race, and great credit is due to the women crews of open cars - Nancy Mitchell, Pat Faichley, Annye Bousquet and others. Mrs.Mitchell and Miss Faichley (M.G. A) were third in their class. Like the Targa Florio and the Tour of Sicily, the Mille Miglia is individual; it is a hark back to the old days of town-to-town racing, it is run over 990 miles of normal public roads, with very fast stretches - as from Ravenna to Pescara where Moss' average last year was 140 m.p.h. - and the slow, winding section up from Viterbo and over the Futa Pass. Crowds line the route, pressing inward as a car goes by

and forgetful of the fact that it may be followed by another. The Mille Miglia is an odd mixture of race and rally. The route, as with a rally, cannot be memorized - a practice lap may last for 12 hours. Opposition to the event has existed in high places, since the present hostile attitude to motor racing arose. Signor Ariosto, of the Italian Ministry of Transport, who was in charge of the commission set up in Italy to investigate the safety measures at the various circuits, has been responsible for the decision to hold

this year's event and a great many steps have been taken to ensure the safety of spectators. Thousands of troops have been stationed round the route to control the crowds and the irresponsible are to be subjected to a fine if they wander.

There is now no question of the later and slower entries finding the roads occupied by everyday traffic; the route is entirely closed until the last car has passed. The entry limit has been reduced from last year's 600 to 400 and, to avoid the overtaking risks for

drivers of the faster cars, the very slow ones have been eliminated and a minimum speed has been set for each class. The cripples will not be allowed to plod along and finish hours late; those who fail to maintain the set average will be flagged off at the next control. Finally, drivers have been accepted only after a thorough examination of their previous record.

Brescia; Sunday, April 19.
For the past three days, since scrutineering began on Thursday, the people of Brescia have de-

cided to abandon their everyday pursuits to enter wholeheartedly into the spirit of motor racing. It holds the town. Strolling crowds, thousands strong and speaking every language in Europe, have swarmed round the cars, pestered drivers for signatures and exposed hundreds of feet of film. Every now and again the roar of an exhaust echoes round the Piazza della Vittoria as an impatient drivers, moving from one scrutineering desk to another, tries to clear a way through the throng. Banners, flags, loudspeakers, model cars in the shops, bright umbrellas outside the cafés with Mille Miglia motifs in red, local enthusiasts who have de-silenced their Vespas and Millecentos for the occasion and roar round the streets - the packed town has caught the motor racing fever and is determined to enjoy every minute of it. Suddenly a car driven by a well-known driver arrives in the square - the crowds swarm across to gaze and proffer notebooks, diaries, programmes, bus tickets...anything on which he can sign his name.

Stirling Moss arrived yesterday, on foot and unshaven, and was immediately engulfed - last year's winner, a valuable signature. For the best part of an hour he patiently and good-humouredly

wrote "S. Moss" for all nationalities.

The new 3 1/2 litre Maserati, despite the efforts of 20 mechanics who had been working on it throughout Friday, could not be completed until 7 a.m. yesterday, when Stirling took it out and climbed the Futa Pass - his first drive in the car. As a precaution, he said, he and Denis Jenkinson were taking their suitcases with them. A new favourite arrives; the crowds are fickle and Moss scuttles away to escape.

So the days of scrutineering have passed and the conversation in the cafés and throughout the town has been confined to the great race. Will Fangio win...Collins, or Moss? Will the fuel tanks of the many, many Giuliettas come adrift as they have been doing in practice... Was it right that the Triumph TR2s should have been compelled to remove their hard tops

and run in the sports class instead of the Gran Turismo? Finally the great moment arrives. Under the glare of the floodlights the first car drives up the ramp on to the 4ft high starting position. The crowds that swarm round the ramp cheer excitedly. Ariosto drops the flag... and, at 11 p.m., away goes Santinello's little Fiat 600 into the night. The others follow, small cars first - Renaults, Fiat-Abarths, Panhards and Morettis, with a preponderence of the little Abarth-converted Fiat 600s-small, 750 c.c.engines with a lot of work to do. Standing on the starters' dais is Renzo Castagneto, "father" of the Mille Miglia, whose bowler hat has been famous since the first race was run. This year the bowler has been forsaken for a trilby.

There are 51 cars in this smallest class - for series production touring, and Gran Turismo, up to

750 c.c. - and they leave at half-minute intervals. The crowds thicken, and the troops try patiently to keep them back. Many of these smaller cars carry only the driver, and one ponders on their next 16 hours or so-driving at racing speeds for near on

1,000 miles with no navigator and only the sparsely sited route markers - and the crowds - to show the way.

In the 1,000 to 1,100 c.c. class there are 45 cars and, of these, 44 are Fiat Millecento-based; the odd man out is a Lancia Appia.

Peter Collins at the wheel of his Ferrari 860 Monza Scaglietti. Below, Eugenio Castellotti with the Ferrari 290 MM Scaglietti.

Next come the 1,100 to 1,300 - with a seemingly endless succession of scarlet Alfa Romeo Giuliettas, and a few Peugeot 203s and Porsches for good measure. So it goes on. A few people drift off to bed, but the majority remain to watch the big cars set off. The night trails by; the long stream of cars comes through...up on to the ramp, into the glare of the lights...pause at the top, and away with a roar and a wave, into the darkness. Gradually the sky lightens and the floodlighting seems less bright; the bigger cars, the likely winners, arrive... the crowds - even bigger now - stir, and cheer...Cesare Perdisa (3-litre Maserati), Eugenio Castellotti (3 1/2-litre, 12-cylinder Ferrari), John Heath, with the H.W.M., Peter Collins, with Louis Klemantaski, recent winners of the Tour of Sicily; Taruffi, strongly favoured in the 3-litre Maserati; Moss and "Jenks" - "barbarossa" - have a tremendous ovation, with cries of "Moos"; Musso and, finally, at 6 a.m., Fangio (3 1/2 litre, 12-cylinder Ferrari) drive on to the ramp to the accompaniment of announcements concerning "il campione del mondo", and the biggest ovation of all.

The crowds disperse; the ramp has served its purpose. From now on, at Brescia and at every town along the route, the leaders at the various controls will be posted up on special hoardings. Crowds wait to see them go up and talk excitedly about the race; the most unexpected people are there-elderly country folk, early in the morning, come to hear the latest progress reports. The atmosphere that was generated here in Brescia is now spreading down to Rome and back again. Meanwhile, news of the race begins to filter through. The early starters have passed through Ravenna, first of the controls, where it is raining; the class leaders are announced. Though the roads on this stretch are generally wide and good the heavy rain makes them slippery. Despite the elaborate safety precautions, Giacobi's 1,900 Alfa has left the road and injured five spectators, two, it was learned, fatally. Gorza's Giulietta, too, has been involved in an accident, the driver escaping with minor injuries but his co-driver is fatally hurt. Sheila van Damm, unhappily, witnessed this accident in her driving mirror. Best time so far recorded from Brescia to Ravenna (through the big cars have not yet gone through) is Cabianca's 100 –

Worse still, Busch's 300 SL has crashed near Pescara, the co-driver, W. Piwko, receiving fatal injuries. Though officially running as private entries, the 300 Sls are works-sponsored and under the wing of Alfred Neubauer. The Stuttgard cars are still a force to be reckoned with.

British cars continue to dominate the class for sports cars with a price limit; Guyot's Jaguar leads, followed by Ronnie Adams' TR2, steadily climbing, Wisdom's Austin-Healey, Bruno Ferrari's A.C., Terragnoli' M.G. A and-Mme. Bousquer's Triumph TR2. After the fast, straight stretches down to Pescara, the diminished field cuts across to Rome – by lesser roads, part made in places, undulating and twisting and traversed by level crossings. The news comes through that, just after Pescara, von Trip's Mercedes has left the road, letting Reiss through into second position in general classification. On they go towards Rome, Castellotti still in the lead, then Reiss, Collins, Muss, Moss, Fangio, Gendebiern, Perdisa, Cabianco and Pollet; Castellotti's average at this stage is 102,85 m.p.h.

By the Rome control Peter Collins has taken second place from the Mercedes-Benz, with an average of 93.25 m.p.h. to Reiss' 92.5. Still ahead is Castellotti's Ferrari, slowed by the twisting section from Pescara at an average of 95.95 m.p.h.

plus m.p.h. in the Osca-with an engine of only 1,500 c.c. – and, in the class for sports cars up to 750 c.c., Chiron's Osca leads Navarro's Panhard, averaging 94 m.p.h. to Ravenna.

Of the largest class, Castelotti's 3 1/2-litre, 12 cylinder Ferrari is comfortably in front by Verona, on the way down to Ravenna, his average to Verona being 120.7 m.p.h. Behind him comes Taruffi (3-litre Maserati), Musso (3 1/2-litre Ferrari), Perdise (3-litre Maerati), Moss (3 1/2-litre Maserati), Fangio (3 1/2-litre, 12 cylinder Ferrari) and Collins (3 1/2-litre, 4-cylinder Ferrari). By Padua – only 50 miles on – the order is Castellotti, whose average has increased slightly, Taruffi, and Moss, followed by Musso, Perdisa, Fangio and

Collins... but these are early stages in the long and arduous event.

In the 1,300-1,600 c.c. Gran Turismo and special series touring class, Sheila van Damm and Peter Harper lie ninth in the Rapier, behind eight Porsches, the second Rapier lying eleventh. In the class for open sports cars costing not more than 2,000,000 lire, British cars are well placed, holding the first six positions-Jaguar, Austin-Healey, Triumph, A.C., M.G., and Austin-Healy. Even at this stage, the struggle for leadership in the general classification is intense. At Ravenna, Castellotti is leading Taruffi by 19 sec, and von Trips' Mercedes-Benz 300SL is 58 sec astern of Castellotti and 39 behind Taruffi. But the Maserati's

brakes, waterlogged in the heavy rain near Ravenna, fail to slow the car for a corner; it leaves the road, the cooling system is damaged and Taruffi is forced to give up. By the time they have reached Pesaro, 55 miles on, Trips is in the lead, his average speed being 107.5 m.p.h. to Castellotti's 107.35. It is short lived, however; by Ancona Castellotti is backin front, with Trips, Reiss (300 Sls) Collins, Fagio, Musso, Moss and Gendebien (2-litre Ferrari Mondial) strung out behind. Madame Thirion's Renault is gallantly tailing Manzon's D.E. in the G.T. and special series touring class up to 1,000 c.c. –averaging over 70 m.p.h. By Pescara, 38 of the 367 starters are out and among them is Leslie Brooke's Austin-Healey.

ANOTHER MILLE MIGLIA WITH MOSS
A TALE OF WOE
BY DENNIS JENKINSON

Some years ago there was a popular ballad entitled "Trees" and the last line ran "… but only God can make a tree".
By the grace of God and one of His trees I am able to write the story of my 1956 Mille Miglia.

But let us go back to the beginning, which for me was shortly after the 1955 Mille Miglia when Moss asked me if I would go with him again, and naturally I said I would. This year we had not got the finance and organisation of Daimler-Benz behind us, in fact we had the complete opposite, provided by Maserati, and a week before the race it was difficult to believe that we were competing. Moss was racing at Aintree, so on the way back from Sicily I did a little reconnoitring of the course and called in at Modena to pick up a practice car and have a look at our "racer", which was to be a new 3.5-litre. The practice car was in use by Giardini, who was somewhere around the 1,000 mile course, and was due back on Saturday, April 21st while there was no sign at all of our 3-litre. However, there was one new car nearing completion, it being destined for Taruffi, and mechanically this new design of chassis, engine and transmission looked pretty good. In every corner of the works were sports Maseratis in various stages of repair and disrepair; there were 2-litre A6G models, 1.5-litre 150S, 3-litre 300S and 2-litre four-cylinder 200S models, varying from a bare chassis frame to a complete car. Rows of engines were being assembled, others were on the test beds being run-in or power-tested, and the activity was obviously going to go on day and night, as it had for some time previously.

Giardini returned with the practice car, a once-pretty coupé A6G with body by Zagato, but now a very weary and dirty-looking motor car, having completed seven laps of

the Mille Miglia course in various hands, it being the only available practice car.

By Sunday morning it had been dusted over and was ready for another lap with Moss and myself, and before taking delivery I went out to the Modena Autodrome, actually the perimeter track of the Modena aerodrome, with the chief mechanic Bertocchi, and he proceeded to put in four very fast laps in the pouring rain to see if all was in order. Everything was, so I set off for Milan airport, the weather still coming down vertically, and I had strict instructions not to exceed 5,500 r.p.m. as the engine was getting tired, and to keep an eye on the oil level, this production engine being wet-sump. On the way to Milan airport, where I was due to meet Moss direct from his lucky win at Aintree, the weather cleared up an I had the opportunity to enjoy this rather pleasant Maserati coupé. Everything about it was pure "racing car", the steering being light and positive, the short gear-lever, operating in an open gate, being a joy to use, though first and second gears were so far apart that it needed a dull pause while changing. Although a very low coupé, the visibility was without criticism and the driving position, even for my dwarf-like stature, was ideal. The brakes were good but tended to

judder badly, though this wore off in time, and the engine was so lively that an eye had to be kept on the rev.-counter all the time to avoid going over the limit, and 5,500 r.p.m. in top came all too easy, equal to 98 m.p.h. When new these engines can go to 6,000 r.p.m., which would give an easy 107 m.p.h. on the rear-axle ratio we had in. There was quite a lot of exhaust noise, but little from the engine and virtually no wind noise from the body, while the smoothness of the six-cylinder engine impressed me enormously. Rather reluctantly I handed the car over to Moss, the only consolation being that I would now be able to see how well it could go, and we returned to Brescia for an early night. On the Monday morning we left Brescia at 5.54 a.m., our starting time in the race, in order to get some appreciation of the sun conditions at that hour. We rather optimistically assumed the sun would be shining, in spite of the rain showers throughout the previous

week. Without exceeding 5,500 r.p.m. (98 m.p.h.), we soon discovered that we were averaging a higher speed round the course than we had done in practice last year with a 300SL Mercedes-Benz when using a maximum of 130 m.p.h., the reason being that the little Maserati was so much more manageable. It could be flicked from side to side of the road with the minimum of effort, and in and out traffic with very little space required, while the gearbox would keep the revs up.

Stopping for lunch after nearly 400 miles, we met Bellucci and Parrella surveying the course in a 1,900 Alfa-Romeo, both having Maserati entries in the race. Bellucci was to drive a new 2-litre four-cylinder in the 150S chassis and his friend a normal 150S. Pressing on again we came to a road block and a long line of traffic, and discovered that we had caught up with the Tour of Italy motor-cycle race, a sort of six-day Mille Miglia for small motor-cycles. Also waiting were

two more Italians practicing in an Alfa-Romeo and the German driver Erwin Bauer, who was in a special Mercedes-Benz 220a. This was outwardly a normal car devoid of bumpers and unnecessary weight, but it was fitted with the new twin-carburetter 220a engine. We arrived at the tail end of the motor-cycle race, so that all we saw were a few stragglers going along at a bare 30 m.p.h., and when we suggested to the police who were guarding the barrier that they let us through, their reply was unanswerable. They said that the road was closed until 3.30 p.m. and that next Sunday when were driving in the Mille Miglia it would also be closed until 3.30 p.m. We would not like it if they let motor-cycles onto our course, and equally the motor-cyclists would not like it if they let cars on today. We went back and sat in the Maserati.

As the time for opening the roads approached the crowd began to get restive, for clearly the last competitor had gone, and there was much shouting that Moss should be let through, but the police were adamant. We got the Maserati up past the queue of traffic, to the head of the line, and there was a bit of "underground" movement by some of the enthusiastic lorry drivers, during which they urged us to make a break for

it and motor off, but the police were not fooled and we had to wait until 3.30 p.m. Then off we went and for the next 50 miles or so the roads were very clear so we had a good dice but were rather piqued to find that a 220a Mercedes-Benz was sitting on our tail, and it took a lot of work to shake it off. The rest of the day's run was uneventful and we got as far as Siena by the time darkness fell, having now developed a very great regard for the 2-litre Maserati coupé, which at first we thought was rather a rough old lot.

Next morning we were off again at 7 a.m., up to Florence and over the mountains to Bologna, the little coupé going really well and crossing the Futa and Raticosa with never a single hesitation. Some idea of how it was going can be gained by the fact that our running time since leaving Brescia would have put us third in the 2-litre Grand Turismo category had we been in last year's race with the car, and this was on open roads, in and out of the traffic.

We arrived back at Modena and went back to the Maserati factory, where Taruffi had just finished testing the first new 3.5-litre car, so off we went to the Autodrome and Moss put in a few laps with the car, but was not very impressed as it understeered rather violently. We wanted to do another lap of the course, and it now being Tuesday we wanted to get off at once, so another car was produced as the 2-litre coupé had to be got ready for the race. It was due to have a new engine, gearbox and rear axle, and some happy Italian was going to race it on Sunday. Bertocchi produced a special two-seater sports car for us, which was an experimental car built in 1954. They had taken a normal A6G two-seater, chopped off the rear of the chassis and fitted the back end of the G.P. car to it, de Dion side-mounted gearbox and all. The steering had been changed to right-hand, and a detuned 2.5-litre G.P. engine fitted. Except for the right-hand drive it looked like a normal 2-litre sports

outwardly, and in 1954 had been driven by Fangio and Marimon in the Supercortemaggiore race at Monza. With this "weapon", for it really was a rather potent piece of machinery, we set off on our second lap, stopping for lunch beyond Brescia and making good time down to the Adriatic, using a maximum of 115 m.p.h. in view of the traffic. In the late afternoon the rain started and we discovered that the Maserati was anything but waterproof, and though the showers were intermittent it rather put a stop to us learning very much and we stopped for the night at Pesaro.

Next morning saw us ready to leave at 7 a.m. but the Maserati became truculent and wetted all its plugs, subsequently needing a tow all round Pesaro before it would run on six cylinders. This was accomplished by an old man in a Fiat Topolino, who was press-ganged into the job by the happy locals who followed us on bicycles, scooters and in cars. By 8 a.m. we were well under way and

singing down the Adriatic coast, but our song was soon cut short for the heavens opened and we were soaked to the skin, and it rained nearly all the way to Rome. Apart from appreciating just how slippery Italian roads can get in the wet, which we knew already anyway, we learnt little on this second lap. By the time we reached Rome we had water in the brakes and also in the kingpins, so that the steering was almost solid and Moss was doing most of the steering with the throttle and the rear wheels. By the time we reached Siena the sun was out but it was not much help and during the afternoon we struggled on our way over the mountains once more, amid streams of traffic, for it was a national holiday in celebration of some victory or defeat somewhere in the distant past. With the Maserati being so low and right-hand drive, Moss discovered a novel way of making "mimsers" move over. He drew up alongside and thumped on the side of their bodies with his fist, the resulting "dong" being audible above the Maserati exhaust, so it must have been devastating inside a travelling tin-box. We got back to Modena rather damp, very dirty and not a little tired, having done 2,000 miles round Italian roads in 2 1/2 days. At least we thought we would be able to try

the new 3.5-litre for size, but there was not a hope, for it was still in the body-builders and there was clearly more than a day's work to do. As the race was getting precariously near we suggested that perhaps we ought to take a 3.5-litre, which was well-proven, and not wait for the new 3.5-litre. At that the technical faces at Maserati fell, for this 3.5-litre was their new baby. It was not a re-hash of the 3-litre, it was all new design, chassis-frame de Dion rear end, engine, clutch, gearbox, transmission, everything was new, but we felt forced to suggest that perhaps it was a bit too new for the Mille Miglia. Then we learnt that Taruffi was not happy with his 3.5-litre and was going to race with one of the old 3-litres, and the Maserati people agreed to prepare another 3-litre for us, just in case. On Thursday we left for Brescia to attend the prize-giving of the 1955 race, it being a tradition of the Mille Miglia that the prizes are given one year after the event. We were up again at 6 a.m. on Friday morning, having agreed to a bed-early-up-early routine for the whole week before the race, and went back to Modena, once more hoping to try our 3.5-litre. It was still in the body-builders and had 22 mechanics working on and around it, so we could not say they were not trying, but it was

nowhere near completed. All day was spent wandering aimlessly round the factory, our spirits sinking lower and lower, and trying to decide whether to take a 3-litre or wait for the 3.5-litre. The technical "bods" kept encouraging us with information about how good the car would be, and by showing us plans for the future both in sports and Grand Prix racing, but we were beginning to wonder. At 11 a.m. we were told it would be ready at 2 p.m., then 5 p.m., then 7 p.m. and when the sun went down we gave up and said we would be back at 5.30 a.m. next morning. When we left the car was still on axle stands, unpainted and not yet run, while four mechanics were working on a 3-litre for us.

Next morning, soon after dawn,

we were back and there was our new 3.5-litre, painted, trimmed and tested, everyone having been up all night, and Bertocchi having taken it round the Autodrome at 3.30 a.m. On the bottom of the radiator air intake a protruding "lip" had been built and there were vague mentions of the front of the car lifting at over 130 m.p.h., but that this would cure it. In order to learn something we had demanded that we took the 3.5-litre and the 3-litre out to the Raticosa mountain and try them in turn over the same piece of the course, and in the early hours of the morning before the race we set off from Modena to Bologna and the mountains, with Bertocchi following in the 3-litre.

We decided to do a timed climb for 10 kilometres up the mountain,

and a timed descent over the same stretch, thus taking in every possible type of corner and gradient. On the way to the mountain we had managed a quick 5,200 r.p.m. in fifth gear, equal to 145 m.p.h., and had found that the front of the car wandered about rather disconcertingly. After three goes up and down the Raticosa, we eventually made the best time with the new 3.5-litre and settled on it for the race, much to the relief of Engineers Alfieri and Colotti. Although quicker from A to B the new car was far from right, having far too much understeer and not responding to anything the driver did to induce oversteer, should he enter a corner too fast. Most cars can be made to break adhesion on the rear wheels, either by using the power, the brakes, the steer-

Other competitors in the special category for open sports cars of restricted prices: the Triumph TR2 of Adams Ronald-McMillen and the Austin Healey 100 S of Brooke and Astbury.

ing or letting the clutch in sharply in a lower gear, but this 3.5-litre refused to respond to any such treatment. The real fault lay in the fact that the new de Dion rear end had made such a vast improvement to the adhesion of the rear tyres under all conditions that the front was now lacking. An understeering car is all right providing you do not overdo things in a corner; if you do then you must provoke rear-wheel breakaway in order to counteract the lost adhesion of the front tyres. Although we agreed to take the new car we were very conscious of the fact that, though its overall cornering power was higher than the 3-litre, it did not allow any margin of error, and in the Mille Miglia the margin of error must be quite high. Leaving the car at the factory for attention to minor details and the fitting of a few home comforts in the cockpit, we set out once more for Brescia, a steady two-hour run from Modena, for it was now well into the morning and we aimed to be in bed by 6 p.m. Maserati were fully appreciative of the shortcomings of the new chassis, but it was too late to alter the geometry of the suspension and reduce the understeer at this late hour. During the afternoon the whole team of cars, 2-litres, 3-litres and in 3.5-litres, arrived at Brescia for scrutineering, and we were greeted

with the unhappy news that our car was making a funny smell at over 120 m.p.h. At 6 p.m., when we had been hoping to retire to bed, we had to take the car out on the Autostrada for a further test. Sure enough, at 120 m.p.h. there was a smell of scorching rubber, but by the time we stopped it had disappeared and nothing could be found amiss, so in a rather unhappy state of mind we retired to bed. The car was geared to do 165 m.p.h. but thus far we had not gone over 145 m.p.h., so we had not only the scorching rubber smell but also the weaving to think about, and in addition it suddenly occurred to us both that the "protruding lip" had been removed without explanation.

Next morning, Sunday, we were up at 5 a.m. and a friend took us out to the start, where the mechanics had the 3.5-litre waiting

and warm, and though the weather was fine team manager Ugolini told us to expect rain within an hour of the start. At 5.54 a.m. we rolled down off the ramp and were away, our number being 554, while Taruffi had 553, Collins 551, Castellotti 548 and Perdisa 547. Though we had tried to cheer each other up by suggesting where we were going to pass them all, we both knew that in reality it was a question of where Musso and Fangio were going to pass us, for Musso was starting two minutes behind us, number 556, and Fangio was number 600, the last away. Before very long I could sense that Moss was far from happy with the car, for he was driving with great caution even on wide open bends, and over some of the humps which I signalled as "flat out" he was easing the throttle. Understeer is a quality that a passenger cannot

feel, and only by watching how far the driver turns the steering wheel for a given corner can one appreciate just how much understeer is being applied. On the limit the initial loss of adhesion is felt instantaneously by the driver, but not until the front of the car fails to change direction is the passenger aware of it. With an oversteering car the passenger can feel every degree of slip-angle that the rear wheels develop and can live with the driver through every corner and situation. Occasionally Moss would give me long glances and it was obvious that the handling was far from pleasant, while on the straights he was working it up to 5,600 r.p.m. in fifth gear (nearly 160 m.p.h.) and the front was wandering in a horrid manner, so I began to realise why he was easing off for some of the flat-out humps. In spite of the faults of the chassis, the engine was running well, and we were making reasonable time, but nothing like record time, and we got to Padova in little over an hour, but, just as Ugolini had warned us, the rain started. Up to now we thought we had been having trouble, but with the rain it really started, for water poured in from under the car and rose between the seats in a heavy spray, so that in addition to the rain beating on us from over the windscreen, we had more rain beating

The Italians Terragnoli and Suppi (MGA) and the Frenchmen Frilloux-Pagot (Triumph TR2) also entered the special category for open cars of restricted price. In the private battle between the two team, the Italians (90th overall) prevailed over the French (only 157th).

upwards from the rear of the seats. In a matter of minutes we were soaked to the skin and under the driving seat there was a good two inches of water. Not content with being that depth it was turbulent as though being beaten by an egg whisk, and as fast as I tried to dry spare goggles for Moss, those he was wearing became useless. Even a car which will run straight at high speed can be trying in the wet, so just how he was coping with this Maserati I could not imagine, yet I occasionally saw as much as 5,200 r.p.m. on the rev.-counter with the gear-lever in fifth. By this time we had passed some of the slower competitors, but naturally had seen no sign of the other

works drivers. On a long straight before Ferrara we were groping our way along at about 130 m.p.h. when Musso went by in his 3.5-litre four-cylinder Ferrari and how he could see we could not imagine, for rain was really coming down now. A bit later, on a winding section, the rain eased off a little and we saw Musso just ahead of us, and this spurred Moss on and he caught and passed the Ferrari, forcing the nose of the Maserati alongside Musso as we approached a corner in a village so that the Ferrari gave way. On another long straight nearing Ravenna we caught up with a 2-litre Ferrari travelling at about 120 m.p.h. and the spray and general derision flying out the back was

fantastic. Nothing we could do attracted the driver's attention, for the road was only wide enough for two cars and he was having to concentrate to stay in the centre. For two or more kilometres we sat in the wake of this car, at times the water even obliterating its red tail, which was only about two feet in front of our car. In a do-or-die effort Moss forced his way alongside, the concrete posts on my side of the road being uncomfortably close, and then we were past and, by comparison, the mere rain seemed like a dry day. The only encouraging thought was that Musso was going to have to go through the same performance, for the road was still straight for miles; not that we wished him any harm. Just before Ravenna we overtook John Heath going very carefully in the H.W.M., though we were not to know it would be the last time we should ever see him. The Ravenna control came and went without a hitch, our card was stamped while we were still on the move, and then away we went again. The roads were like ice-rinks in places, and in some of the towns the cobblestones were so slippery we had to cross them on a trailing throttle, for to accelerate

would have spelt disaster. Down to the Adriatic coast we went, the rain never ceasing and we were now so wet that cold was beginning to set in, in spite of the heat from the engine coming through the bulkhead. Our nice neat tin of biscuits and fruit was full of water and the food was a messy pulp, while I looked at our drinking bottles of orange juice and smiled to myself, for we must have drunk a gallon of rainwater already and I felt sure it was beginning to seep through the pores of my skin. We were wearing waterproof clothing, but we might just as well have been sitting naked, and had we been on a stripped chassis we could not have been wetter. I looked at Moss as he peered into the rain and wondered what it is that makes a driver carry on under such circumstances, for apart from all the physical discomforts there was the added mental strain of knowing that he had little or no safety limit with the car should he overdo a corner, while over some of the humps it gave some really horrible wavers on the front end. But still he battled on and, when I realised that all the other drivers were suffering from much the same problems, I saw the Mille

The AC Bristol of Bruno Ferrari and Franco Dari at the start.

Miglia in its true light and began to get a glimmering of why people race in it and why they were refusing to give up. All along the road we were seeing wrecked cars, some in ditches, others upside down, another with its nose through a wall, one so far off the road in a field it was difficult to see how it would ever get out again. I began to realise that this was not a motor race, it was something far greater, far tougher - it was a battle between the human race and all those things its agile brain had schemed up. Here was Man trying to prove to himself that the machines he made, the roads he built, the houses, the walls, the bridges, everything he had constructed were for his use and that he was master of them all, but Nature was putting up her best opposition and everything that Man had made with his own brain and hands was now conspiring to kill him. If we gave up now it would be admitting defeat by our own devises. I could see that we must go on, we must fight our way through; this was not a battle of one man against another, it was an impossible fight of Man against himself, and if he gave up now the human race was going to lose some of its reason for its existence.

It was only under such terrific pressure that the human being

could satisfy itself that it was master of the earth. This was more than a motor race, we were not racing against Musso or Castellotti or Fangio; it seemed that we were fighting for the mere right to go on living. Maybe we were not good enough to win this battle, but others would be, and I felt that whoever was leading this greatest of all battles must go on to the bitter end, no matter how many fell by the wayside. Knowing racing drivers as I do, I was sure that some of them would fight their way through, and I could see clearly perhaps for the first time, just why a man drives a racing car in competition.

Shortly before Fano, on another long straight, Musso came by again, and we just could not hold on to him, but later on, after Senigallia, we saw him by the roadside, and our first thought was that he had broken the car. However, we saw that he was relieving his bladder, for to race with it full is to risk serious internal injury in the case of a slight bump. As we neared Pescara, the rain stopped and a feeble sun tried hard to break through the clouds, and for

the last 20 minutes before reaching Pescara the roads were almost dry, but we were still sodden. In front we saw a 3-litre Maserati and, though we were doing 5,600 r.p.m. in top gear, we were gaining nothing on it along the straights. After a few corners we got close enough to recognise the yellow helmet of Perdisa, but in spite of our extra 1/2 litre we could not overtake him on the straight. After some more villages we closed on him and sat in his slipstream right into Pescara, outbraking him for the S-bend over the level crossing and arriving at the control and our first refuelling stop just in front of him. In spite of both Maserati cars arriving together the mechanics did an excellent job of work and both tanks on our car were filled quickly and we were away again. The pit had told us that we were fourth in our class, but only sixth overall, the fantastic von Trips being second in his 300SL and Castellotti leading all the way.

Barely five minutes out of Pescara, heading for the Abruzzi mountains, the rain started again, and once more there was some goggle

changing and cleaning to do for the driver, and now we had Perdisa on our tail. All the way to Popoli we passed and re-passed, but as we soared up into the mountains on our way to Aquila Moss began to throw the Maserati about a bit more and we shook Perdisa off, though it was obvious that the 3-litre was proving far more easy to handle on the wet and slippery road. On one bend we had seen the 300SL of von Trips, off the road and facing us, with all the front smashed in, and we hoped he was not hurt, while up in the mountains we came across a 1,900 Alfa-Romeo well and truly jammed into the retaining wall. By Aquila, the rain had stopped once more, but for only a few minutes, for as we started the descent down towards Rieti it began again, and this time in real earnest, with clouds almost down to road level. Just before Rieti is reached the road descends down the mountainside, in a series of quite fast bends, to the village of Antrodoco, which lies at the very foot of the mountains. On our way down this descent we had one really big slide, during which it was

122

pretty obvious that Moss had lost
complete control, but by sheer
luck the car stopped sliding before
we had used up the width of the
road. With only four kilometres to
go to the foot of this mountain descent we entered a right/left gentle
ess before rounding a sharp right-
hand bend, all downhill. Everything
was going fine, apart from the torrential rain, and as Moss entered
the S-bend on a straight line
across the apex, he braked, ready
for the sharp right-hander. The
next few moments were some of
the fullest I have ever spent.
For a fleeting moment the front
wheels locked on the slippery
road, and that was that, all adhesion on the tyres was lost and the
car slid helplessly across the road
towards the right-hand bank. With
a resounding crash we hit a small
stone wall, bounded over it and
began to mount the earth bank on
the right of the road. By good fortune, the car was still going
straight and we tore down a
barbed-wire fence, and then I realised we were some 15 feet
above the road, at 45 degrees to
the horizontal, and I was convinced the car would now roll over
sideways, for I could see Moss
way above my right shoulder. In-
stinct, or motor-cycle training,
made me curl up and keep my
arms tucked out of the way, and
then I felt the car retain the hori-

zontal once more and I remember
thinking with relief that it was not
going to roll over after all. I looked
up just in time to see that we were
now plunging down the end of the
bank, then there was a fleeting
glimpse of the road and in front of
us was a black-and-white concrete retaining wall of post and
rails, on the outside of the sharp
right-hand bend. I ducked, there
was a loud bang, a jolt, and the
car had stopped. All was silent,
except for the horn, which was
blowing loudly. With some relief I

realised that at least we were not
on fire, for I was very conscious of
the large petrol tank alongside my
seat. As we came to rest I heard
Moss yelling "Get out, quick", and
saw him leap from the car. I got
out quickly and fell flat on my face
among shrubs and grass, and together we scrambled away from
the wreckage, all the while the only sound being the long single
note of the electric horn and
steady beat of the pouring rain.
We made sure that neither of us
was hurt and then cautiously went

back to the poor battered Maserati
and switched off the main electric
circuit, which stopped the noise of
the horn and left only the noise of
the rain. The car had come to rest
nose first against a tree about 15
feet from the road, but down a 60-
degree grass slope. As we
climbed back onto the road we
heard cars approaching and saw
Musso and Perdisa go by, and
waved to them that we were all
right. Then we walked back and
surveyed the path of our uncontrollable flight, from the moment
we lost adhesion on the front
wheels. We found the first wall we
had hit was about 12 inches high,

123

and it was on that impact that I realised that our Mille Miglia was over. Then we looked at the tracks along the 45-degree bank and realised that had we been going slower we would never have travelled the whole length and would have certainly finished upside down in the road. At the end of the bank we had flown off a 3-ft wall and made contact with the retaining wall on the outside of the bend without touching the road, for neither of us remembered feeling a bump as we landed. Then Moss felt that he had a scratch on his right cheek, and we found that the barbed-wire had made a tiny line just below his right eye. When we found the windscreen scratched, the glass of the watch which he wears on his right wrist, and the glass of his goggles and his helmet also scratched, we realised how very close to a nasty injury he had been. Then we looked over the edge of the road and immediately at each other, both thinking the same thoughts. The Maserati was resting nose first against the only tree for many yards around, and

beyond the tree the 60-degree slope went on down for 300 feet to a boulder-strewn river bed at the bottom, with nothing stronger than small bushes in the way.

IT WAS AT THAT MOMENT THAT I REMEMBERED THE BALLAD "TREES".

The whole incident had started at about 70 m.p.h. and had taken some 200 yards to exhaust itself, and the fact that neither of us had anything broken or bruised was just one of those lucky breaks that keep some people alive. There was nothing we could do about the car, so salvaging spare goggles, our route book and a solitary banana, we set off to walk to Antrodoco, some 3.5 kilometres farther down the mountainside. Just then we heard a Ferrari approaching, and it could only be Fangio, so we stood on the side of the road and gave him a "thumbs up" sign and, bless his dear old Argentinian heart, he stopped to ask if we were all right and then offered us a lift in his passenger seat to the next town. We waved him on, indicating that

he was supposed to be racing, but he smiled and shrugged, and indicated that he was in no hurry and was "touring" to finish. Fangio is too old and wise to hurry in impossible conditions - he obviously had no intention of doing himself any damage. "The Master" knows when and where to go fast. We continued to splash our way down the road and after a time we met some of the locals coming up, they having seen the car appear over the edge of the bank from below. Our return to Brescia was a long and tedious process and, but for keeping a sense of proportion and humour, it would have been a misery. A competitor in a 1,900 Alfa-Romeo stopped and gave us a lift to the outskirts of Rome, where a spectator took us in a Fiat 1,400 to a hotel. We were both looking very bedraggled and shivering with cold and wet, and the hotel manager was rather taken aback at our demand for a room and a bath at lunch time. Eventually we got our circulation going again, had a meal and rang the Maserati agent in Rome. In quite a short time he ar-

rived with some dry clothes and, packing our sodden racing gear into brown-paper parcels, we took a taxi to the station. There were five minutes to spare before an express left for Bologna and as I watched Stirling Moss standing at the ticket office, buying two singles to Bologna, wearing a borrowed suit and raincoat, with a brown-paper parcel tied with string under one arm, and his crash-hat and goggles under the other, I roared with laughter, for this was really the funniest way to finish the Mille Miglia, especially remembering how we had finished last year's race. On the train we heard that Castellotti had won the race, and we paid tribute to outstanding courage and skill. By 9 p.m. we were at Bologna and telephoning Moss' mechanic Alf Francis, who was staying at Modena, and he came out in the Vanguard to collect us. Our troubles were not over yet, for the continuous rain had swollen the rivers and the main road was flooded. The police sent us off on a 20-mile detour which ended at a bridge that had been washed away, so we returned to the main road and after lots of yelling and shouting we splashed our way through the floods. Taking turns at driving we arrived back at Brescia at 2.30 a.m., and we crept into the hotel and to bed feeling happy to be alive but so tired it was

Motor Sport, June, 1956

THE XXIII MILLE MIGLIA

A Personal Triumph for Castellotti

In spite of popular alarums and excursions the Mille Miglia took place on April 28/29th in exactly the same form as past years and the only differences in the route were two new by-pass roads: at Pineto, on the Adriatic coast, and San Quirico, shortly before Siena.

Of the 427 entries, only 54 failed to turn up in the Piazza Vittoria in Brescia for the official scrutineering, leaving 373 cars, ranging from Fiat 600 to 3.5-litre works Ferraris, and between the finish of scrutineering on Saturday afternoon and 11 p.m. that night, when the first car left the starting ramp in the Viale Rebuffoni, heading east for Verona, another eight failed to report. As is tradition, the small cars left first, beginning at half-minute intervals; at 11.37 p.m., when the first Fiat 1,100 left, the intervals were enlarged to one minute, the cars getting faster and more powerful as the hours wore on. By the time the really fast cars left it was daylight, Fangio being last away at 6 a.m., though many of the fast 1,500-c.c. sports cars and the big Gran Turismo models had left in the dark.

Along the fast straights to Padova the day was fine, though the sky was cloudy, but before Rovigo and the crossing of the River Po, rain was falling heavily. As far as the eye could see the sky was heavy with rain and the fast open cars were being severely handicapped, so at the first control at Ravenna it was not surprising to find two Mercedes-Benz 300SL cars on the leader board. Castellotti (Ferrari) was in the lead, with Taruffi only a few seconds behind him, and then came von Trips and Riess, both profiting from closed cars and efficient windscreen wipers. Most impressive was the performance of Cabianca with the little 1,500-c.c. Osca, who was lying fifth ahead of such opposition as Moss, Collins, Musso, Gendebien and Perdisa, to say nothing of his team-mates Villoresi and Maglioli.

Reaching the Adriatic coast at Rimini, von Trips was going at an enormous pace, and by the time he reached his first refuelling stop at Pesaro he was actually leading Castellotti by a few seconds. Taruffi had water in his brakes and failed to stop at one corner, the resulting excursion into the undergrowth damaging his radiator too badly for him to continue. Castellotti had refuelled at Ravenna and he regained the lead while Trips refuelled, but they clocked in at the control at Pescara with only two minutes separating them, a truly creditable performance by both German car and driver. All the drivers of open cars were having great difficulty with visibility for it was raining heavily all the time until a few minutes before the Pescara control, when there was a slight break. Riess was backing up his 300SL team-mate splendidly, keeping ahead of Collins and Fangio, the high-

speed sections down the coast road having been too much for the little Osca and it had dropped back. On the twisty road from Pescara to Popoli von Trips was following an Alfa-Romeo saloon into a bend when it braked suddenly and the SL driver had to take violent avoiding action which resulted in his car spinning round and crashing through a concrete barrier, fortunately without injury to driver or mechanic. By this one slight error on the part of another driver the German's fine drive came to an end, and this let Riess up into second place. Castellotti was driving the race of his life, alone in the 12-cylinder Ferrari, and was unassailably in the lead at Aquila, while Collins had moved up into third place and Musso and Moss had ousted Fangio from the leader board over the mountainous section in the Abruzzi. Shortly after this, still in torrential rain, Moss went off the road and smashed the new 3.5-litre Maserati, and Musso dropped back behind Fangio. Off the mountains at Rieti the way was still treacherous and the rain continued to pour down, but Castellotti was making no mistakes and driving at great speed but with a remarkable surefootedness.

At Rome he was still in the lead, nearly 10 minutes in front of Collins in a four-cylinder Ferrari,

with Klementaski as passenger, as on his winning drive in Sicily. On the hard twisty part of the course up from Rome, over the Radicofano mountain, where the clouds were down on the road, Collins could make nothing on Castellotti, though equally the leader could not draw away, and at Firenze they were still approximately 10 minutes apart. Riess failed to arrive at the Firenze control on time and he dropped right back, letting Musso and Fangio by first of all and then, as he slowed, Gendebien went past into fifth place and leader of the Gran Turismo category with the works 3-litre coupé Ferrari. The Scuderia Ferrari were now having a clean sweep, being in the first five places in the general category, and the order was to remain unchanged right over the Apennines and along the fast straights back to Brescia and the finish. Over the Futa and the Raticosa the rain was continually teeming down and cloud and mist brought visibility down to a bare 50 yards, yet still Castellotti made no mistakes. He is usually reckoned to be rather wild in his driving but he was now disproving this idea, and throughout the whole 1,000 miles he never put a foot wrong, arriving home a very wet and tired winner, but having accomplished a magnificent feat. With the ap-

palling weather his average was naturally low by Mille Miglia standards, though fantastic in view of the conditions, while he made history by being in the lead at every control point, losing it only momentarily between Ravenna and Pescara.

In a race the size and complexity of the Mille Miglia it is naturally impossible to follow the fortunes of every competitor, nor is it possible until many weeks after the event, when the detailed times at all the controls have been tabulated, to follow closely the changes in leadership in all the various categories. However from various sources and information gleaned from competitors it is possible to gather together a word-picture of various sections of the vast entry and to record some of the happenings that overtook many of the cars and drivers. Quite naturally it would be possible for the driver of a 600 Fiat to have enough excitement in 1,000 miles to fill a whole magazine,

while the faster the cars the more likely there is to be incidents and hazards.

MILLE MIGLIA MUSINGS

Among the 1.5-litre sports cars the Osca team ran into fuel pump troubles, both Villoresi and Maglioli having to fiddle with the electrics to make any progress at all. Maglioli finally gave up the unequal struggle at Bologna and left the car at the factory, returning to Brescia to pick up his personal 300SL.

Giulio Cabianca's win in the 1.5-litre class was well deserved as he specialises in open-road racing and has been faithful to Osca for some years now.

Hans Herrmann was a favourite in the 1.5-litre class with the new works Porsche Spyder but had valve trouble at Aquila. Fortunately he had Werner Enz, a factory mechanic, with him and they were able to remove the valve gear from one cylinder and return home on three cylinders the fol-

lowing day. Bracco in the other factory Porsche, a 1955 car, found the brakes inoperative in the wet and decided to retire before he did any damage.

Jean Behra finished 20th overall and second in the 1.5-litre class with a 150S Maserati, driving in his first Mille Miglia. He might have won the class had not a rear-brake pipe split. Feeling that only the front brakes were working he pressed on, but eventually all the fluid leaked away and he had no brakes. Stopping at a wayside garage he made up a new brake pipe himself, the mechanics all being on holiday watching the race, and fitted it. To do this he had to remove the spare wheel, which necessitated a certain amount of "forcing" - like on so many Italian cars the spare wheel was larger than the boot lid. After bleeding the brakes he was able to continue but had lost some 45 minutes all told.

Among the 2-litres Bellucci had to retire the works four-cylinder 200S models with lack of brakes due to water, while Giardini relaxed his driving of an A6G and let Scarlatti win the class with a similar car. Among the drivers of six-cylinder Maseratis were many newcomers, some of them going terribly slowly.

Among the big cars poor John Heath crashed in the H.W.M.

The departure of the unfortunate John Heath who left the road in his HWM near Ravenna and later died in hospital of the injuries he sustained.

near Ravenna and later succumbed to his injuries in Ravenna hospital.

Leslie Brooke crashed his Austin-Healey, but without serious injury, and Tommy Wisdom finished the course in his works car, though behind the works M.G.s.

Without doubt the Prima Donna of the event was Nancy Mitchell who drove the entire race herself, taking Pat Faichney for company. The MGA was standard and fitted with two tiny aero-screens, so that both girls were soaked to the skin. Nancy had never been round the course so that all the time new and interesting terrain opened up before her. Rally experience in mountain country where you must drive on reflexes made the journey possible and she finished 74th. In addition, they were the first all-women equipe to finish and fifth in the 1.5-litre class, not so far behind Scott-Russell and Haig in a similar car. Whereas Nancy Mitchell's rally M.G. tended to fall apart immediately after leaving the start, the Mille Miglia car never missed a beat and behaved impeccably throughout.

The Belgian girl-wonder Gilberte Thirion continued her remarkable exploits driving a Renault Dauphine on her own and finishing before such mere males in similar cars as Trintignant, Rosier

and Frere, though it must be allowed that the last named looped-the-loop with his during the 1,000 miles.

The French girl, Annie Bousquet, who refused to give up racing no matter what the setbacks, drove a Triumph TR2 and was so wet and cold that for the last part of the race she was unable to change gear. She had some energy pills in the pocket of her overalls but was too stiff and cold to get them out. Such will-power deserves a special medal. Under such circumstances many men would have given up.

One of the most outstanding performances was that of Sgorbati with one of the new Sprint-Veloce Alfa-Romeo Giuliettas in finishing 11th in the overall category. He was followed by Becucci driving a similar car, while Swedish driver Bonnier was 15th with yet another Sprint-Veloce.

The Ferrari 250 Europa coupé which won the Gran Turismo class was a typical sports/racing coupé. So much water leaked in that it could have used a wiper on the inside of the windscreen. Gendebien had anything but an easy drive, going off the road four times and spinning round three. His passenger, Jacques Washer, was still smiling happily at the end.

Both Sunbeam Rapiers finished unscathed, Peter Harper and Sheila Van Damm sharing the driving of the factory car. That production Sunbeams, M.G.s, Triumphs, Jaguars and Austin-Healeys all finished the course goes to show that it is possible to screw English cars together properly, and that they are not such big heaps of junk as many people imagine. One thousand miles in less than a day over Italian roads, including four mountains, is a

good enough test for anybody. The next step is to produce some more speed and to finish amongst the 12th to 20th places - among the Alfa-Romeo Giuliettas, Porsche Carreras, 300SL and Lancia Aurelia.

First all-British combination to arrive at the finish was the MGA of Scott-Russell and Haig, who were 70th.

A pity that the British pair Collins and Klementaski could not have won, thus making a double with the Giro Sicilia. With four factory Ferraris in the over 2-litre class and finishing 1-2-3-4 the Scuderia Ferrari made history. Fifth place by the Gran Turismo factory Ferrari completed the grand slam.

The new 750 c.c. Osca cars had a sweeping victory, for though Chiron was put out by a seized ball-race in the clutch when he got to Pescara, he was way out in the lead of the class. From there his team-mate Cappelli went into the lead and won by over 30 minutes from Stanguellinis, which normally dominate this category.

In the touring 750 c.c. class the win by Michy in his little Renault was most praiseworthy, for his average speed was not only higher than that of Manzon in the Gran Turismo D.B. coupé, but also of the fastest Fiat 1,100, while the

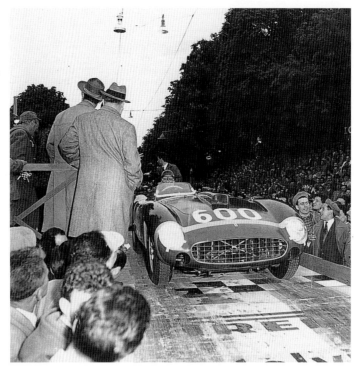

souped-up Fiat Abarths were well and truly beaten up by the long-established French car. Tales of remarkable achievements, hair-raising incidents and arduous drives could go on forever, for with 365 cars having left the start and only 178 arriving back at the finish in time to qualify, the mechanical mortality can be imagined. Four drivers reached Brescia after the maximum time allowed for their particular category, and one of these, in a 1,900 Alfa-Romeo saloon, was completing his 14th Mille Miglia. He had little or no interest in dicing, being quite content to tour round the course and add another Mille Miglia to his list. Being an Italian, his real satisfaction came from driving for a whole day on roads he knew well without having to dodge bicycles, dogs, lorries and other traffic. That alone must be paradise to an Italian.

When the XXXIII Mille Miglia finished it was still raining and it must have been the toughest on record, a complete contrast from last year's race, during which the sun shone throughout. Whereas the 1955 race was a triumph for Mercedes-Benz and Stirling Moss, the 1956 race was truly a personal triumph for Eugenio Castellotti.

NOTES ON THE CARS IN THE MILLE MIGLIA

In the over 2-litre class the issue lay between Ferrari and Maserati, and the Maranello firm entered two 12-cylinder, 3.5-litres as used in the Giro Sicilia, to be driven by Castellotti and Fangio, and two four-cylinder 3.5-litres, similar to the Sicily winning car, to be driven by Musso and Collins. There were no radical changes to them, and only Collins carried a passenger, the others having the left side of the cockpit covered and a single wrap-round screen. From Maserati came three works entries, Perdisa and Taruffi with 3-litres as raced in Argentina and Sebring, the only modifications being the fitting of enormous fuel tanks in the passenger seat, and one new 3.5-litre Maserati started, in the hands of Moss, it being a brand new car both in design and construction. The engine of 86 by 100 mm. bore and stroke was 3,485 c.c. and while still a six-cylinder was not an enlarged 3-litre, but an entirely new design as far as castings, portings and so on were concerned.

Unlike the 3-litre, this new engine had the carburetters mounted horizontally and not slightly downdraught, while the magnetos were mounted on the rear of the camshafts. On the back of the clutch was a step-down pair of gears not only lowering the prop-shaft line but also reducing the speed of the shaft. This drove to a new unit-construction gearbox/differential unit, containing five speeds, all of which could be used. The gearbox part of the final drive unit was in the front of the axle line, whereas the 3-litre and G.P. cars have the gearbox on the side of the differential. With the new layout the de Dion tube had to pass behind instead of in front of the final-drive and a vast improvement was made by locating the central guide of the tube directly to the rear cross-member instead of on to the final drive casting. The new frame was of the space type, using fairly large diameter tubing as on the 3-litre and G.P. cars but was of a different formation. The rear suspension still used a transverse leaf-spring, mounted

high above the rear end, but the de Dion tube location was on an extension below the tube itself. At the front the well-tried double wishbone and coil spring layout was retained, but both front and rear were fitted with telescopic shock-absorbers in addition to the normal vane-type Houndaille. New front brakes as large as those on the G.P. cars were fitted and 3-litre-type rear brakes. A great deal of thought had gone into the layout of the rear suspension and the construction and the whole car was rather heavy as it was intended for a bigger engine than 3.5 litres, which has yet to be finished. In the tail of the car was a 40-gallon fuel tank and the oil tank, while on the left of the cockpit was another fuel tank of 18 gallons. As on the 3-litre the steering was right-hand drive, the column feeling its way between the three double-choke Weber carburetters by means of universal joints. This new 3.5-litre engine was claimed to give over 270 b.h.p. at 5,800 r.p.m. and to be possessed of excellent torque characteristics.

Among the private owners in this class were Bordoni and Gerini with normal 3-litre Maserati, Heath with the H.W.M.-Jaguar, Graham with the XK120 Jaguar,

and some early privately-owned Ferraris.

The 1,500-c.c. to 2,000-c.c. class of sports cars was almost a Maserati benefit, there being six-cylinder A6G models driven by good drivers, bad drivers and indifferent drivers, among the first group being Scarlatti, Giardini and Pucci, while Bellucci had one of the new 150S models fitted with a 2-litre four-cylinder engine, this differing outwardly from the 1.5-litre four-cylinder only in having larger-choke carburetters which were mounted at a slight downward angle. Against these were some 2-litre Ferraris, both four-cylinder and 12-cylinder, the only serious opposition being the new four-cylinder Sbraci, this being a small version of the Monza Ferrari to look at but having a non-de Dion rear end, suspended on 1/2-elliptic springs.

The 1,100-c.c. to 1,500-c.c. group was more interesting, having factory entries from Maserati, Alfa-Romeo, Osca and Porsche. Behra was in a 150S Maserati, virtually as sold to the public, but with a few detail modifications and quite a bit more power; Sanesi was driving a hotted-up Alfa-Romeo Giulietta Spyder open two-seater; the Osca team was as raced in Sicily, being Villoresi, Maglioli and Cabianca; and

there were two Porsche cars from the factory. As Frankenberg was not able to be in Italy his entry was taken by Bracco, the car being one of the 1955 Spyder models, but the other was a brand new car making its first appearance and driven by Herrmann. This had a small-diameter tube space-frame and aluminium body, the rear no longer hinging upwards about the extreme end, but having hinged panels on each side for getting at the carburetters and the air grilles on the top of the tail hinged for access to the rear-axle-details. Any major work necessitated unbolting the whole tail of the car from the cockpit rearwards. Front suspension and brakes were unchanged but the engine was much modified and fitted with a five-speed gearbox but not with the low-pivot swing-axle that Porsche have been ex-

perimenting with. In addition to these works entries there were privately-owned 150S Maseratis driven by Cornet, Bourillot, de Tomaso, Petralla and Michel. All these were the standard models, rather solidly made and heavy in the chassis by English standards, but Maserati pointed out that the chassis was designed to take a 2 1/2-litre engine and still not break up over 1,000 miles of Italian roads, including the rough mountain passes. The chassis frame on these cars is built up from fairly large oval-section tubing and small round-section tubing to form a peculiar structure that is neither "ladder-type" nor space-frame, but a complicated mixture of the two. The front suspension is by wishbones and coil-springs, but there is no normal kingpin as on the Grand Prix cars. The point of each wishbone forms a pivot

for rotational and up-and-down movement, and into this fits a very short kingpin, one top and one bottom, and these are part of the stub-axle forging. The rear suspension is de Dion with a transverse leaf-spring mounted low beneath the whole assembly, with the tube located centrally on a sliding joint, the attachment to the tube being on a bracket welded below the tube itself, to give a lower roll centre. The four-cylinder engine remains unchanged from the proto-type which appeared at Nurburgring last year, having two double-choke Weber carburetters, eight plugs and two overhead camshafts. The four-speed gearbox bolts onto the rear of the engine and an open propeller-shaft drives to the differential unit mounted on the rear of the chassis frame. Right-hand steering is utilised and a full-width aluminium

Results:

MILLE MIGLIA-Italy-1,597 kilometres-Conditions Very Wet

* 1st: E. Castellotti (Ferrari 3.5-litre 12-cyl) 11 hr. 37 min. 10 sec. - 137.442 k.p.h.

2nd: P. Collins/L. Klementaski (Ferrari 3.5-litre 4-cyl) 11 hr. 49 min. 28 sec.

3rd: L. Musso (Ferrari 3.5-litre 4-cyl) 12 hr. 11 min. 49 sec.

4th: J.M. Fangio (Ferrari 3.5-litre 12-cyl) 12 hr. 26 min. 50 sec.

* 5th: O. Gendebien/J. Washer (Ferrari 3-litre 12-cyl) 12 hr. 29 min. 58 sec.

6th: P. Metternich/W. Einsiedel (Mercedes-Benz 300SL) 12 hr. 36 min. 38 sec.

7th: W. Siedel/H. Glockner (Mercedes-Benz 300SL) 12 hr. 38 min. 24 sec.

8th: J. Pollet/Flamdrack (Mercedes-Benz 300SL) 12 hr. 49 min. 58 sec.

* 9th: G. Cabianca (Osca 1.5-litre) 12 hr. 57 min. 11 sec.

10th: F. Riess/H. Eger (Mercedes-Benz 300SL) 13 hr. 06 min. 31 sec.

* 11th: R. Sgorbati/Zanelli (Alfa-Romeo Giulietta S.V.) 13 hr. 06 min. 42 sec.

12th: G. Becucci (Alfa-Romeo Giulietta S.V.) 13 hr. 12 min. 41 sec.

Class winners

Class Results:

Special Touring, 750 c.c.:

1st: M. Michy (Renault 4 c.v.) 14 hr. 34 min. 55 sec. - 109.519 k.p.h.

2nd: A. Thiele/A. Storzini (Fiat Abarth 750) 15 hr. 05 min. 54 sec.

3rd: R. Cotton (Panhard) 15 hr. 10 min. 20 sec.

Special Touring, 1,100 c.c.:

1st: R. Scarfiotti (Fiat 1,100) 14 hr. 39 min. 15 sec. - 108.979 k.p.h.

2nd: D. Fania/M. Maggio (Fiat 1,100) 14 hr. 51 min. 44 sec.

3rd: E. Mandarini/Bertassi (Fiat 1,100) 14 hr. 52 min. 48 sec.

Special Touring, 1,300 c.c.:

1st: M. Stern/R. Barbey (Alfa-Romeo) 13 hr. 47 min. 50 sec. - 115.726 k.p.m.

2nd: R. Martin/H. Convert (Alfa-Romeo) 13 hr. 49 min. 49 sec.

3rd: G. Acutis (Alfa-Romeo) 14 hr. 08 min. 54 sec.

Special Touring, 1,600 c.c.:

1st: D. Lissmann (Porsche 1,600 c.c.) 14 hr. 08 min. 04 sec. - 112.986 k.p.h.

2nd: P. Harper/Miss Van Damm (Sunbeam Rapier) 15 hr. 04 min. 37 sec.

3rd: W. Wisnewski/F. Bosmiller (Sunbeam Rapier) 15 hr. 22 min. 01 sec.

Special Touring, 2,000 c.c.:

1st: M. Toselli/F. Caneparo (Fiat) 13 hr. 19 min. 20 sec. - 119.874 k.p.h.

2nd: D. Pistoia (Alfa-Romeo 1,900) 13 hr. 45 min. 49 sec.

3rd: B. Mazzi/E. de Amicis (Alfa-Romeo 1,900) 13 hr. 48 min. 22 sec.

Special Touring, over 2,000 c.c.:

1st: E. Bauer/E. Grupp (Mercedes-Benz 220a) 13 hr. 42 min. 20 sec. - 116.522 k.p.h.

2nd: Nataloni/Passerini (Lancia Aurelia) 14 hr. 03 min. 23 sec.

3rd: S. Heurberger/W. Heurberger (B.M.W. 502) 14 hr. 21 min. 50 sec.

Gran Turismo 750 c.c.:

1st: D. Ogna (Fiat Abarth) 16 hr. 48 min. 06 sec. - 95.050 k.p.h.

2nd: A. Linguanti/Bocchio (Fiat Abarth) 16 hr. 57 min. 43 sec.

3rd: M. Poltronieri/A. Villiger (Fiat Abarth) 18 hr. 07 min. 18 sec.

body and with only the driver in place the left side of the cockpit is covered by a metal panel and a wrap-round windscreen is used.

The sports class, from 750-c.c. to 1,100-c.c., is the home of amateur-built "specials", early 1,100-c.c. Oscas and privately-owned models from the small firms like Stanguellini and Ermini.

In the 750-c.c. class there was some factory support in the shape of two very beautiful little 750-c.c. Osca four-cylinders with twin overhead camshafts, being scaled-down versions of the factory 1.5-litre cars; these being driven by Chiron and Capelli. Against these were Le Mans-type D.B. and Panhards, and special Renaults from France, Stanguellinis, Giaurs, etc.

There was one more open sports class, seemingly specially designed to allow the British to win something, and it was for open cars costing not more than 2 million lire (1,150 pounds approximately) and of catalogue specification. This attracted two works M.G. MGA models driven by Nancy Mitchell and Scott-Russell, another Italian-entered one, a Porsche Speedster, Triumph TR2, A.C. Ace, Jaguars and Austin-Healey 100S models, and a lone Spyder Fiat 1,100.

In the over-2-litre Gran Turismo class Ferrari entered a factory car driven by Gendebien this being a

12-cylinder 3-litre, of which over 100 have now been made, with wishbone and coil spring i.f.s. and 1/2-elliptic-sprung normal rear axle, and a very solid "vintage-like" chassis. It was fitted with a small coupé body by Scaglietti, a coachbuilder in Modena. There were some private models of this type entered, but the real opposition came from Mercedes-Benz with 300SL models. Private owners were Siedel, Zampiero, Busch, Metternich, Pollet, Mascaranhas, Cacciari and Bongiasca, all receiving attention and advice from the factory, represented by Neubauer and Kling and a handful of mechanics. In spite of their announcement to the contrary there were two factory-entered cars driven by Riess and Graf von Trips. These still had to be to catalogue specification, but were nevertheless full factory entries. The competition springs and shock-absorbers were available to these drivers as well as to the private owners, but Trips decided he preferred the standard soft springing controlled by competition shock-absorbers. Mixed in with this class was a group of cars entitled Special Series Touring and this included three special Mercedes-Benz 220a models, stripped of unnecessary weight and having twin-carburetter engines, special camshafts and so on, and were driven by

Gran Turismo, 1,100 c.c.:
1st: R. Manzon (D.B. Panhard 850) 14 hr. 36 min. 13 sec. - 109.356 k.p.h.
2nd: A. Massari/P. Gatti (Fiat 1,100) 15 hr. 13 min. 37 sec.
3rd: Mlle. G. Thirion (Renault Dauphine) 15 hr. 14 min. 10 sec.

Gran Turismo, 1,300 c.c.:
1st: R. Sgorbatti/Zanelli (Alfa-Romeo Giulietta S.V.) 13 hr. 06 min. 42 sec.
121.799 k.p.h.
2nd: G. Becucci (Alfa-Romeo Giulietta SV) 13 hr. 12 min. 41 sec.
3rd: J. Bonnier/B. Boenson (Alfa-Romeo Giulietta S.V.) 13 hr. 20 min. 58 sec.

Gran Turismo, 1,600 c.c.:
1st: P. Persson/Blonquist (Porsche Carrera) 13 hr. 32 min. 54 sec. - 117.874 k.p.h.
2nd: M. Nathan/G. Kaiser (Porsche Carrera) 13 hr. 40 min. 07 sec.
3rd: F. Kretchmann/K. Trager (Porsche Carrera) 16 hr. 12 min. 53 sec.

Gran Turismo, 2,000 c.c.:
1st: M. Maggiorelli/A. Parenti (Fiat 8V) 13 hr. 33 min. 03 sec. - 117.852 k.p.h.
2nd: N. Sassoli/Schon (Fiat 8V) 13 hr. 38 min. 12 sec.
3rd: M. Guarnieri/D. Brancalion (Fiat 8V) 13 hr. 44 min. 57 sec.

Gran Turismo, over 2,000 c.c.:
1st: O. Gendebien/J. Washer (Ferrari 250) 12 hr. 29 min. 58 sec. - 127.765 k.p.h.
2nd: P. Metternich/W. Einsiedel (Mercedes-Benz 300SL) 12 hr. 36 min. 38 sec.
3rd: W. Siedel/H. Glockler (Mercedes-Benz 300SL) 12 hr. 38 min. 24 sec.

Sports, 750 c.c.:
1st: O. Capelli (Osca) 15 hr. 41 min. 15 sec. - 101.800 k.p.h.
2nd: P. Martoglio (Stanguellini) 16 hr. 15 min. 32 sec.
3rd: P. Faure (Stanguellini) 16 hr. 16 min. 27 sec.

Sports, 1,100 c.c.:
1st: A. Brandi (Osca) 14 hr. 48 min. 42 sec. - 107.820 k.p.h.
2nd: E. Manzini/C. Chiarel (Ermini) 15 hr. 33 min. 16 sec.
3rd: C. Falli (Osca) 16 hr. 12 min. 25 sec.

Sports, 1,500 c.c.:
1st: G. Cabianca (Osca) 12 hr. 57 min. 11 sec. - 123.264 k.p.h.
2nd: J. Behra (Maserati 150S) 13 hr. 34 min. 09 sec.
3rd: H. Sauchen/Bialas (Porsche) 14 hr. 50 min. 14 sec.

Sports, 2,000 c.c.:
1st: G. Scarlatti (Maserati A6G) 13 hr. 19 min. 02 sec. - 119.919 k.p.h.
2nd: F. Giardini (Maserati A6G) 14 hr. 38 min. 42 sec.
3rd: J. Gottgens/P. Rouselle (Triumph TR2) 15 hr. 15 min. 07 sec.

Sports, over 2,000 c.c.:
1st: E. Castellotti (Ferrari 3.5-litre) 11 hr. 37 min. 10 sec. - 137.442 k.p.h.
2nd: P. Collins/L. Klementaski (Ferrari 3.5-litre) 11 hr. 49 min. 28 sec.
3rd: L. Musso (Ferrari 3.5-litre) 12 hr. 11 min. 49 sec.

Sports Cars of Limited Price:
1st: G. Guyot (Jaguar XK120) 14 hr. 07 min. 15 sec.
       113.095 k.p.h.
2nd: H. Sauchen/Bialas (Porsche Speedster)
       14 hr. 50 min. 14 sec.
3rd: P. Scott-Russel/T. Haig (M.G.A)
       15 hr. 02 min. 17 sec.
Total starters: 365. Total finishers: 178.

G.P. of Nuvolari
(fastest time Cremona-Mantova-Brescia - 134 kms) :
E. Castellotti (Ferrari), 46 min. 49.8 sec. - 169.122 k.p.h.

Index of Performance: M. Michy (Renault).

Positions of noted British teams: 2nd: Collins/Klementaski; 70th: Scott-Russell/Haig; 72nd: Harper/Van Damm; 74th: Mitchell/Faichney; 77th: Wisdom/Monaco; 150th: G. Grant.

Gunzler, Retter and Bauer, all three being factory sponsored. This grouping of Gran Turismo and Special Series Touring applied for all capacities, the 1,600-c.c. to 2,000-c.c. class containing the limited-production A6G coupé Maserati models, Alfa-Romeo Sprints, Fiat 8V and the hotted-up versions of the 1,900 Alfa-Romeo and Fiat 1,900. The 1,300-c.c. to 1,600-c.c. group saw Porsche Carreras, the two valiant Sunbeam Rapiers, one driven by Sheila Van Damm and Harper, and an M.G. Magnette driven by Grant. The 1,100-c.c.

to 1,300-c.c. group contained an enormous collection of Alfa-Romeo Giulietta Sprints and the new Sprint-Veloce version, this being outwardly the same, but having aluminium doors, bonnet and boot lid, Perspex sliding windows, normal floor-mounted gearlever, twin double-choke Weber carburetters, different camshaft and compression ratio and an ability to rev to 7,000 r.p.m. It was a very serious attempt to beat the 1,300 Porsche Supers, of which only a few were entered this year. The 750-c.c. to 1,100-c.c. group was sub-divided at 1,000-c.c. so

that the upper group was entirely Fiat 1,100 with the exception of one poor little Lancia Appia, and the lower class saw D.K.W., Renault, D.B. and Panhard meeting. There were five of the new Renault Dauphines, those of Trintignant, Rosier, Frere and Gilberte Thirion being special factory models with highly-tuned engines. In the up-to-750-c.c. class there

were Panhard, Renault, Fiat, Moretti and Abarth, the last-named being special modifications of Fiat 600. Outwardly they were unchanged but the engine had an increased bore and stroke to bring it up to 750-c.c., new crankshaft, camshaft, larger carburetter, improved manifolding, and about the performance of a normal Fiat 1,100 TV.

*1) Eugenio Castellotti being interviewed before the start of the race.
2) Marino Guarnieri and Brancalion won the 2000 cc class of the TS and GT group of the Nuvolari GP.*

Following the heavy 1955 defeat at the hands of the Mercedes, Ferrari placed five cars in the first five places in the overall classification. Eugenio Castellotti won with the 290 MM (1) and also took the Nuvolari GP and the Campari GP awards for the fastest times over the Brescia-Rome and Rome-Brescia sections. Second overall were Peter Collins and Louis Klementasky (2) with the four-cylinder Ferrari 860 Monza.

1

*Luigi Musso with the Ferrari 860
Monza (1) finished 3rd ahead of
Juan Manuel Fangio with the other
Ferrari 290 MM (2) and Olivier
Gendebien and Jacques Washer
with the Ferrari 250 GT (3), the
winner of the GT category.*

2

3

In the Turismo Speciale category victory went to Gilberte Thirion with the Renault Dauphine (4) in the 1000 cc class; Stern and Barbey with the Alfa Romeo Giulietta SV (1), surprisingly included among the Turismo Speciale cars, won the 1300 class; Sheila Van Damn and Peter Harper with the Sunbeam Rapier (2) in the 1600 cc class and Miro Toselli and Franco Canaparo in the 2000 cc class with the Fiat 8V Zagato (3), another surprising inclusion in the category that dominated with an average speed of 119.874 kph. The over 2000 cc class was won by the Mercedes of Bauer and Grupp.

Among the production Gts, Domenico Ogna scored a class win with the Abarth 750 (1), whilst Massari and Gatti took the 1150 cc sub-class with this Fiat 1100/103 TV Pininfarina spider (2), beaten in the category by the Giulietta Svs. The fastest of the latter was driven by Sgorbati and Zanelli (3) who also won the Nuvolari GP. Persson and Blomqvist won the 1600 cc class with the Porsche Carer (4), whilst Maggiorelli and Parenti took a Fiat 8V with frontally modified coachwork to victory in the 2-litre class.

In the category reserved for open sports cars with restrictions on retail prices, the Porsche 356 A Speedster (1) of Saucken and Bialas won the 1600 cc class, Gottgens and Rousselle won the 2-litre class with the Triumph TR3 (2) and the Jaguar XK 140 (3) of Guyot took the special category overall at an average speed of over 113 kph.

The 750 cc class of the Sport Internazionale class was won this time round by an Italian car, the OSCA 750 (4) of Ovidio Capelli, with the Stanguellini of Paolo taking the Nuvolari GP (5).

1

3

2

5

4

1

2

3

4

5

With the exclusion of that of Ovidio Capelli, the results in the other classes of the Sports Internazionale category were modest, partly as a result of the terrible weather. Attilio Brandi won the 1100 cc class with the OSCA Mt4 2AD (1) at an average speed of 107.820, no less that 12 kph slower than Capelli. Giulio Cabianca won the 1500 cc class with the OSCA Mt4 1500 (2), whilst Giorgio Scarlatti drove a hectic final section with the Maserati A6GCS/54 (3) to take the 2-litre class with a time similar to that of Capelli, but both were soundly beaten by the more powerful Maserati 300 S (4) of Cesare Perdisa, first home in the 3-litre class. The Austin Healey 100 S of Tom Wisdom and Monaco (5) won the 3000 Sport class in the Nuvolari GP at an average speed of just 136.121 kph, battling with the Zagato 1100 of Merlo and Facetti.

1

The Porsche Carrera (1) of Nathan and Kaiser won the 1600 cc class in the TS and GT group of the Nuvolari GP at an average speed of 145.713 kph, whilst the Mercedes 300 SL (2) of Wolfgang Seidel and Helm Glöckler won the TS and GT group Nuvolari GP overall (average speed 168.022 kph) as well as the "Giornale di Brescia" GP awarded to the team with the least time difference between the Brescia-Rome section and the return leg to Brescia.

2

TARUFFI WINS MILLE MIGLIA WITH 4.1-LITRE FERRARI

Collins Retires with Victory in Sight: Fatal Accident to De Portago Involving Spectators

From Grande Vitesse.

Brescia, Sunday Midnight. The twenty-fourth Mille Miglia Race here on a spring day of sunshine began with a Homeric battle among Ferrari drivers led by Peter Collins at a speed only fractionally under the Moss record in 1955 and ended under the grim shadow of disaster when within 50 miles of the finish the Marquis de Portago and his American passenger Gunnar Nelson, crashed into the crowd. Both men were killed and several of the spectators were fatally injured-unconfirmed reports up to midnight quote the death toll as 12.

Stirling Moss on what was undoubtedly the fastest car on the course finished his race three minutes after starting when his brake pedal snapped but he was able to pull the 4-5 litre Maserati up without damage. With Behra a non-starter Maseratis had lost the race at the outset and it became a struggle between members of the Ferrari team. Leading all the way with an increasing margin to within 150 miles of the finish. Collins retired giving the victory to Taruffi on a similar 4.1-litre V-12 Ferrari, who had followed him all the way.

Once again the great and ancient city of Brescia set in the Lombardy plain under the shelter of

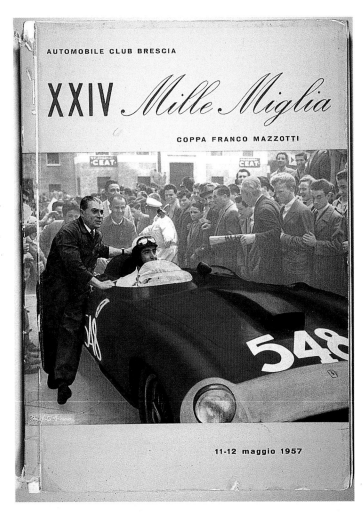

the Northern Alps awoke to the annual carnival of speed which is the setting for the start and finish of the Italian 1.000 Miles Race, the 24th Mille Miglia, which is in direct descent from the epic city-to-city races that were the birth of motor racing.

For days before the race the main square of the city became the paddock where cars were pushed from enclosure to enclosure for the scrutineering surrounded by milling crowds of Bresciani, who always seem to be able to take time off from their usual occupations to gaze in delight at the cars which were so soon to be careering round Italy at high speed. It merely sufficed for the loudspeakers to announce that Stirling Moss was sitting at a café table to start a concerted rush of hundreds brandishing bits of paper for his autograph until he and his fiancée fled the place.

As usual, practising was not without incident. Jean Behra crashed his V-8 4.5-litre Maserati and injured a wrist, robbing the team of a formidable member on the eve of the race. Von Trips (Ferrari) hit a motorcyclist. De Portago wrote off his personal Ferrari; Gregor Grant had to spin his Lotus to avoid a child. Tommy Clark was less fortunate, he overturned his A.C. Aceca in a ditch when girls on a scooter suddenly turned across

Piero Taruffi, with his wife Isabella, assaulted by photographers and filmmakers following his victory. On the facing page, below, Piero Taruffi with his Ferrari 315 s at the start of the race.

his bonnet, but the car was repaired in time for the race. Dick Steed broke a half-shaft on the Cooper-Jaguar while garaging it and a new one was fabricated by enthusiastic local mechanics in time for the race. Ron Flockhart's Jaguar, the 1956 Le Mans-winning car, lent for the occasion by its present owner, had to have a new gearbox flown out.

Ten Gears for Moss

Maserati were left with only one 4.5-litre V-12 for Moss. Fitted with a dual ratio giving him five high and five lower speeds, a car in which he was quietly confident, for its power is enormous - capable of over 200 m.p.h. An entirely new model was given to Hans Hermann, a V-12 of 3 1/2 litres, and the new driver, Giorgio Scarlatti, had the familiar 3-litre 6-cylinder model. Fangio, of course, had not entered for this race. Against them the Ferrari attack was prodigious with two V-12 4.1-litre cars for Collins, passengered by photographer Klemantaski, and the veteran Pierro Taruffi, supported by von Trips and the Marquis de Portago on new 3.8-litre 12 cylinder models derived from the 3.5-litre. Two of the Fitzwilliam team of four M.G. As had disc brakes. Blakesley's and Carnegie's.

Contrivances which served as the now-obligatory hood were in many cases highly amusing. Some had no fastenings: one was attached to the radio aerial and another was made of what looked like cellophane. A curious feature this year was the outbreak, as yet not epidemic, of advertising on some of the cars, a thing usually regarded as an anathema by the F.I.A., the governing body, except in the United States. Mrs. Nancy Mitchell after a delayed flight from the Tulip Rally arrived to find her Triumph TR3

hard-top listed in the wrong class, but the matter was corrected, placing her machine with the standard models. She was again partnered by Miss Pat Faichney. The two Sunbeam Rapiers (Miss Van Damm and Peter Harper), class winners last year, had engines slightly bored out within the permitted tolerance, more power than ever, larger brake drums and wider linings and air channels to the rear shock absorbers (an Alpine Rally trick) and overdrive. Tommy Wisdom's Austin-Healey 100-6 was removed from the out-and-out sports-car class and

placed more properly with the Grand Tourers. The start for the 301 cars began as usual at 11 p.m. on Saturday night in the wide boulevard of the Via Rubuffone. The night was cool, windless, with an overcast sky. Putting the race back into the second week of May seemed to ensure a dry road. Thousands of spectators and hundreds of soldiers and police milled around the big grandstands under blazing arc lights for the TV cameras. Strings of electric bulbs danced among the fresh green leaves of

the trees. The queue of gleaming cars to be sent off one by one in their classes stretched away up the road, and high up on the blue-and-white ramp glittering in the brilliant illuminations was the first car, Pola's little 750 Fiat. At 11 p.m. down went the flag, the cars burst into life, flashed down the ramp and away up the road past a sea of faces into the distance - the Mille Miglia had begun, and by the time the unlimited sports cars left at 5 a.m. in bright sunshine the small cars were already nearing Rome 500 miles away.

In the sports-car class over 2 litres the private entries were dispatched first-Flockhart's Jaguar D-type followed by Steed's Cooper-Jaguar, the gigantic white-and-blue American Chrysler-engined 400 h.p. Special of Miller and Harrison from California, impassive under enormous blue and white helmets, and Muro's big B.M.W. Then came a pause of a few minutes and the factory cars went off - Scarlatti's 3-litre Maserati; de Portago and von Trips with 3.8-litre Ferraris. Hermann's 3.5-litre Maserati, Collins on one 4.1-litre Ferrari, Taruffi on

the other, and last of all, amidst tremendous excitement, Stirling Moss and bearded Dennis Jenkinson as navigator in the 4.5-litre Maserati.

Moss went quite gently then opened throttle and shot away, reaching some 170 m.p.h. in the first three kilos. Then, approaching a curve at about 120 m.p.h., some seven miles out on the fast stretch to Verona, he braked and the pedal snapped off. The crowd swayed back as he took the corner 20 m.p.h. faster than he had intended, sliding broadside and brakeless. It is reported that several by-

standers remarked that this year Moss was indeed hurrying. After some three minutes of racing he was out and it took 20 minutes to drive the car back to Brescia. The hand brake had no effect whatever.

Ferrari Struggle

At the start the race became a battle between von Trips and Collins, with Taruffi on their tails. The Englishman was through Verona at 118,6 m.p.h., 10 seconds in the lead, the German second, Taruffi third, de Portago fourth - about 45 miles in under 21 minutes.

On the facing page, the arrival of Piero Taruffi, preceding by a second the identical car driven by von Trips who had started three minutes earlier.

At Padua von Trips led by half a minute at 121.3 m.p.h. - staggering speeds on ordinary roads where in every village the crowd jammed the pavements and left a tunnel of human flesh to be aimed at by the drivers at over 170 m.p.h.

Von Trips led at Ravenna (188 miles) by 36 seconds at 116.2 m.p.h., 10 m.p.h. faster than Castellotti last year, and now Ferraris were in first four places, made up by Gendebien on the Gran Turismo V-12 3-litre. Europa model and Bordoni's 2-litre Maserati sixth.

Miss Van Damm (Sunbeam Rapier) crashed near Verona unhurt, skidding off the tramlines into a house. Steed's Cooper had brake trouble after a 120 m.p.h. run to Verona. A Mercedes burst a tyre, another broke down and a third crashed. At Ravenna Vidille's D.B. had averaged 82 m.p.h., a Porsche 90 m.p.h., in which class Harper on the Rapier lay 10th Mrs. Mitchell (Triumph TR3) was fourth in her class, Gendebien and three more Ferraris led the unlimited Gran Turismo class at 107.8 m.p.h., and in the 1500 sports class Maglioli's Porsche led at 103 m.p.h. Carnegie, Fitzwilliam, Hogg, Simpson, Sparrowe and Spiers on M.G. As, holding fourth to ninth places in the class.

Collins Ahead

Near Forli, Collins passed von Trips into the lead with the long 190 m.p.h. straights of the Adriatic coast still ahead when the unlimited class order was: Collins, von Trips, Taruffi, de Portago. Scarlatti and sixth, Flockhart's Jaguar (10th in general category).

By Pesaro, where the fastest section of the 990-mile course begins, Collins led at 112 m.p.h. by 1 min. 24 sec., Taruffi passed von Trips into second place, de Portago fourth, Gendebien fifth, Scarlatti sixth and Flockhart now seventh in general category. At

Ancona, 50 miles later, Taruffi, always regarded as a possibile winner in this race if his car lasts, carved 21 seconds off Collins' lead, drawing away from von Trips by two minutes and averaging nearly 114 m.p.h.

On and on they raced, all teammates together, with no interference now from Maseratis, over the level-crossings, through the villages with their walls of faces, on and on, and at Pescara (386 miles from the start) Collins led at 116 m.p.h. by a clear 53 seconds from Taruffi, and when they turned off the sea coast plain into the mountains of the Abruzzi

Collins increased his lead. At Aquila, 62 miles farther on, he led by 3 min. 7 sec. at 113,5 m.p.h., and as they thundered into the outskirts of Rome 542 miles from Brescia, his lead had gone up to 5 min. 27 sec., 107,26 m.p.h. - over 10 m.p.h. faster than Castellotti last year and only nine seconds slower than Moss' Mercedes record in 1955.

Order at Rome (542 miles)

General Category: 1, Collins (4.1 Ferrari), 5hr. 3 min. 11 sec., 107,26 m.p.h.; 2, Taruffi (4.1 Ferrari), 5hr. 8 min. 38 sec.; 3, von Trips (3.8 Ferrari), 5 hr. 12 min. 31 sec.; 4, de Portago (3.8 Ferrri), 5 hr. 17 min. 43 sec.; 5, Gendebien (3-litre Ferrari G.T.), 5 hr. 17 min. 46 sec.; 6, Scarlatti (3-litre Maserati), 5 hr. 36 min. 8 sec.; 7, Maglioli (1500 Porsche), 5 hr; 37 min. 6 sec.; 8, Luglio (2-litre Ferrari Sport), 5 hr. 44 min. 13 sec.; 9, Munaron (2-litre Ferrari Sport), 5 hr. 46 min. 35 sec.; 10, "Ippocrate" (2-litre Ferrari G.T.), 5 hr. 47 min. 50 sec.

1,500 c.c. Sports: 1, Maglioli (Porsche), 5 hr. 37 min. 6 sec., 96,5 m.p.h.; 2, Schiller (Porsche), 5 hr. 59 min. 59 sec.; 3. Berger (Maserati), 6 hr. 20 min. 26 sec.; 4, Saucken (Porsche), 6 hr. 36 min. 16 sec.; 5, Carnegie (M.G. A), 6 hr. 37 min. 50 sec.; 6, Pagani (Alfa

Romeo), 6 hr. 45 min. 34 sec.; 7, Fitzwilliam (M.G. A); 8, Hogg (M.G. A); 9, Simpson (M.G. A). 2-litre Sports: 1, Munaron (Ferrari), 93.6 m.p.h.

At Rome Mrs. Nancy Mitchell's TR3 was missing and in that class (at this stage the Touring and Grand Touring Classes were, as usual, combined, to be separated only at the finish), Travagliani (Fiat) led at 82 m.p.h., and the elderly Frenchman Morin's Triumph lay fifth.

After a stop for fuel Collins shot off again and at Viterbo, 70 miles on, he led Taruffi by seven minutes at 106 m.p.h., and it seems probable that the team control had now frozen the positions of the triumphant Ferraris.

Another 60 miles to Siena and Collins still increased his lead over Taruffi. North they flew to the valley of the Arno and Florence, Collins now 8 min. 31 sec. in the lead at 98 m.p.h. (last year it was 86 m.p.h.), with the team in formation behind him as they stormed the serpentine curves of the Futa Pass over the Apennine backbone of Italy and down the far slopes to Bologna. On the descent of the Pass a light rain turned to snow, making the winding road into a skating rink, bringing speeds down appreciably and on the approach to Bologna, Collins heard an

ominous noise in the back axle. At the control he had stretched his lead to nearly 11 minutes at an average of just over 98 m.p.h., followed by his teammates as before. After a refuel and wheel change he shot off again, with the race in the bag, knowing that now Taruffi could not catch him. What he did not know was that.

Taruffi also heard a grinding noise in the back axle. Mile by mile the groaning noise in Collins' car grew worse and at Parma, 40 miles farther on, his magnificent drive came to an end.

Taruffi now took up the lead, changing gear as gingerly and as rarely as possible. Through Cremona he stormed with von Trips close behind and in Mantua, the last control, the German passed him - not into the actual lead, however, as he had started minutes before Taruffi. Taruffi of course repassed and in that order they tore down the boule-

vards and across the finishing line two lengths apart to make an impressive demonstration. White-haired Taruffi, the victor by 3 min. 1 sec. at 94.83 m.p.h., 10 hr. 27 min. 47 sec. after he had started that morning and his axle still functioning.

Catastrophe at Mantua

Then the shadow of catastrophe suddenly darkened the day. Coming behind in fifth place, fast out of Mantova on a long straight, de Portago crashed. A bulletin stated a tyre burst, a driver reported he saw a wheel and half-shaft at the side of the road. Whatever happened, the car zig-zagged from one side of the road to the other and then ploughed into the crowd. De Portago and his passenger, the American Gunnar Nelson, who drove with him last year when he won the Tour de France, were both killed, and it is reported that several of the crowd lost their lives. No official announcement

has been made tonight regarding the numbers involved, but it is believed there were 10 or 12 fatally injured.

As the last cars limped home and darkness fell, news began to filter through concerning some of the missing. Mrs Mitchell's Triumph, high in its class, had bounced at a level crossing near Pescara, hit straw bales and damaged the radiator. Tommy Clark's A.C. split its tank and had to be topped up 14 times besides being pushed half a mile to a filling station.

Fitzwilliam's M.G. glanced off a tree and went through a whisky advertisement hoarding which damaged its nose, after which the car was difficult to control but the rest of the team finished, two unscratched: Carnegie's fourth in its class and Peter Harper's Rapier provisionally second in his class. Flockhart's drive ended about half distance with fuel feed trouble, and Grant's Lotus, second in its class.at Bologna, split its tank. The huge Chrysler Special likewise crept home very late. An Italian private owner with an M.G. A, straight from the showroom, finished faster than it started. So a magnificent race ended nearly 10 m.p.h. quicker than last year but clouded by the grief which has stopped all rejoicing tonight.

WITH MOSS IN THE MILLE MIGLIA

BY DENNIS JENKINSON

Our starting time was 5.37 a.m. and our number 537, the last car to start in the 1957 Mille Miglia. For the previous three mornings we had been out on a practice run from Brescia to Padova, leaving the start at the race time, so that when we went along to the Viale Rebuffione at 5.15 a.m. on Sunday morning and took our place in the queue leading to the starting ramp we were both feeling on top of the world. The "four-five" Maserati was all set to go, we had given it a thorough testing under all conditions and it was far more potent that the SLR with which we had set the race record in 1955, so that when team-manager Ugolini told us that the weather was perfect to Pescara and looked like staying so for the rest of the day we both felt confident that we could improve on our 157 k.p.h. average. With Behra a non-starter we had two minutes to wait after Taruffi left, at 5.35 a.m.; then the flag fell, we trickled down the ramp, opened up in bottom gear and as all 400 b.p.h. took hold we fairly shot off up the road into the avenue formed by the milling throng of spectators.

We had barely left Brescia when I sensed that the big V8 engine was buzzing round at 7,000 r.p.m., and a glance across at the rev.-counter showed this to be true, but then I swallowed hard as I saw that Moss was pulling out the overdrive gear, which was acting as a sixth speed, and we were up at 6,700 r.p.m. in overdrive fifth gear. This two-speed gearbox between the engine and the rear-mounted regular five-speed box was a crafty "gimmick" that Maserati had schemed up specially for the Mille Miglia, so that we were geared in the super-top ratio for 285 k.p.h., which we estimated to use on rare occasions, and here we were doing 272 k.p.h. (approximately 168 m.p.h.) just as we were leaving town, on a straight of barely two kilometres. We looked at each other and grinned, for this was acceleration that was a new experience and, with dry roads and the sun covered by light cloud, everything was on our side.

We had covered 12 kilometres when we slowed down from our 270 k.p.h. cruising speed for a couple of sharp right-handers and then we went into an 80 m.p.h. left-hand bend, with an approach speed of about 130 m.p.h. I was conscious of the driver changing down and checking the car with the brakes, and then it seemed to accelerate and I saw that he was deliberately sliding the car into the side of the corner as we approached and my first thought was that it had jumped out of gear. This thought was heightened when I saw him make a violent grab at the gear-lever while the car was sliding across the corner, and then he stopped working on the wheel and we slowed up. I thought, "Well, go on, then, accelerate," but he didn't and I looked sideways to see him pointing to the floor; looking

The ill-fated Alfonso de Portago paired with Edmond Nelson at the start with his Ferrari 335 S. Their race ended tragically at Guidizzolo.

The Chrysler-powered "Caballo de Hierro Mk II" (Iron Horse Mk II) driven by the Americans Miller and Harrison who retired early in the race.

down, I swallowed hard for there were only two pedals on the cross-shaft, an accelerator and a clutch pedal, the brake pedal was lying on the floor amongst the pipes and rods, and I then re-alised why Moss had gone into the corner about 15 m.p.h. too fast ...

It was surely the shortest and sharpest Mille Miglia anyone has ever done; there was no question of going on for the pedal arm had broken off about one inch above the cross-shaft and the hand-brake was about as useful as a sports-car "regulation hood". You can't drive a 400-b.h.p. 25-cwt. two-seater without brakes and hope to keep up with anyone, so we had nothing to do but retire on the spot. Before the race we had been joking about ways and means of retiring early in the Mille Miglia and what it must feel like; now we knew. About the only way we shall beat our 1957 record retirement is to fall off the side of the starting ramp in 1958! Had such a breakage occurred on a British car there would have been harsh words and rudery in the Press, as it was an Italian car

there was some pretty lurid shouting and yelling, but most people, including ourselves, were almost speechless. The reason for such a stupid failure on a brand new car was hard to justify and can only be blamed on a flaw in the metal tube that forms the brake-pedal arm. Even so it was completely and utterly inexcus-able, for closer study showed that it had started to fail at least two days before the race, but though we were annoyed about the whole affair we had to commiser-ate with Maserati for they had put everything they had into this 4.5-litre and for the first time ever there had been a good certainty of a Maserati win in the Mille Miglia, a thing that has not yet happened, for that "four-five" is a fabulous performer.

XXIV MILLE MIGLIA
Ferrari Sweep the Board
Once Again

Brescia, Italy, May 12th
As with many big motor races, the 1957 Mille Miglia resolved in-to a straight fight between the Scuderia Ferrari and the Scude-ria Maserati. This being a sports-

car race both teams brought out their big guns and there was every prospect of a real dice over the 1,597 kilometres of Ital-ian roads that constitutes the sin-gle lap of the Mille Miglia course. After the Sebring race Ferrari looked at his 3.5-litre V12 en-gines, with their four o.h.v., and decided that he needed more horsepower if his drivers were going to cope with the 4.5-litre V8 Maseratis, also with four o.h.c., for the Trident car was giving an honest 400 b.h.p. and proving unbelievably reliable. The two weeks before the Mille Miglia saw Modena and Maranello hard at work on their cars for this tough race, while drivers were circulating Italy in all manner of vehicles, learning the roads and conditions. Every now and then the Via Emilia, which runs through the centre of Modena from Bologna and is part of the course, would have its normal civilian pandemonium shattered as a Ferrari or Maserati, with its trade plate number hastily paint-ed on the tail, would scream away into the middle distance. Sometimes these two-seater

Grand Prix cars, looking like sports cars, would head for some long straight to try and dis-cover top speed, or be taken up into the mountains beyond Bologna, to sort out suspen-sions, gear ratios, brakes and handling. All the while at both factories, almost night and day, the test-houses would be emit-ting the bellowing of the big V8 or the scream of a V12. Although the outright win obvi-ously lay between Ferrari and Maserati, there was going to be a total of 300 competitors sub-divided into numerous cate-gories and classes, so that simi-lar activity was going on in Bologna at the Osca factory, in Modena at Stanguellini, in Milan at Alfa-Romeo, in Turin at Lancia and Fiat and so on, while cars from other countries were being prepared and arriving in Italy dai-ly. Jaguar, Porsche, Renault, Ford, Sunbeam, M.G., Peugeot, even a special from America were all coming over the border for this most fascinating of the classic races, and one of the last remaining town-to-town races. When the final list of starters was drawn up Ferrari entered four 12-cylinder cars, all with the en-gines enlarged since Sebring. Collins, with Klementaski as navi-gator, had a 4,1-litre, Taruffi rely-ing on his fantastic knowledge of

Right, the Cooper Jaguar of Steed and Hall who retired before reaching Rome, as did Ron Flockart (bottom) at the wheel of an Ecurie Ecosse Jaguar D-type.

the roads, had a similar car, von Trips relying solely on his natural ability, having a 3.8-litre and the fourth car being driven by de Portago, with his friend Nelson as navigator. This fourth works Ferrari should have been for Musso, but he was still unwell and certainly not fit enough to race for 1,000 miles non-stop. In a Gran Turismo 3-litre V12 "Europa" were that remarkable pair Gendebien and navigator Washer, and though not in the sports class everyone was going to keep an eye on them in the General Classification. From Maserati were entered two of their fabulous 4.5-litre cars, a

brand new one for Moss, who was being navigated by Jenkinson, and the Sebring-winning car for Behra. These two monsters were to carry all the Maserati hopes for putting up a fight against Ferrari, but in addition there was a new experimental car for Herrmann to drive. This was a 3-litre chassis fitted with a new V12 engine of 3.5-litres, it being an enlarged Grand Prix en-

gine, made from the Grand Prix castings, but having a larger bore and longer stroke. To the casual eye this unit was a Grand Prix engine of the type tried-out at Syracuse early in the season, and this experimental car also had a new five-speed Grand Prix gearbox and carried brakes from the 4.5-litre Maserati. A fourth car was a normal 3-litre 300S, with the big front brakes from the "four-five" and was to be driven by Scarlatti. Maserati also had 2-litre cars in the hands of Bordoni, Bellucci and Pagliarini, in direct opposition to the new 2-litre Testa Rossa Ferraris of Munaron, Sbraci and Koechert. Also in the big sports-car class were Flockhart with and Ecurie Ecosse D-type, Steed with his Cooper-Jaguar, the Americans Miller and Harrison with their 6.5-litre Chrysler-engined "hot-rod" special, and the start was so arranged that these private-owners left before the works entries, with a gap of five minutes between the two groups, so that the works drivers would have a clear run at the opening stages.

Naturally, there was as much rivalry in the other classes, especially among the Gran Turismo cars, such as the Giulietta Alfas and Porsches, but it was nice to se a great number of British cars joining in the fun of these lower classes. Two Sunbeam Rapiers with engines enlarged to 1.5-litre and fitted with extra equipment such as larger fuel tanks were being driven by Miss Van Damm/Humphrey and Harper/Reece, Nancy Mitchell had a TR3 hard top, Wisdom a six-cylinder Austin-Healey, Riley/Meredith with a warmed up Zephyr, Gregor Grant with a Lotus 1,100, Clark with an Aceca, and the Fitzwilliam team on M.G.s. While there is no British manufacturer capable of challenging Ferrari and Maserati for an outright win in the Mille Miglia, the efforts of individuals to break up Italian monopolies in the various minor categories deserves every possible credit.

During the Thursday and Friday before the race the main square in Brescia was a scene of rising animation as touring and grand

touring cars went through scrutineering, followed by many of the sports cars of the smaller capacities. But it was Saturday morning that saw excitement reach its highest point when first of all the Maserati team arrived and then the full Ferrari team. By lunchtime Saturday, Brescia and the surrounding districts could barely contain themselves with excitement, and after the last Ferrari had been scrutineered there was comparative quiet about the place, but nevertheless the air was alive with a fantastic expectancy.

With only 301 starters this year, the first man was not sent away until 11 p.m., but once he had left there was a continual stream of competitors leaving the starting ramp and setting off on 1,000 miles of dicing on normal Italian roads, adequately guarded and closed to normal traffic. At the last minute there had been two upsets. Firstly, Behra had an

accident while out on test with his 4.5 Maserati, and though he was lucky to escape with only a broken wrist and cuts and bruises, he was unable to start. Another unfortunate was Cabianca, who blew up the engine of the works 1,500 Osca after scrutineering, so at the last moment he took the 950 c.c. car which should have been driven by Morolli. This was especially unfortunate as the 1,500-c.c. class was all set for a big battle between Cabianca and Maglioli, the latter driving a works Porsche RS Spyder. Apart from them being in the same class they were due to start one minute apart, which would have really stirred things up. With this change it meant that both Cabianca and Maglioli were almost sure of a class win, for the opposition to two such champions of open-road racing was negligible. With Behra a non-starter all the Maserati hopes rested on Moss with the

other "four-five", for Herrmann's car was very experimental and Scarlatti could not hope to compete against the might of Ferrari with a 3-litre Maserati.

Barring accident, the outright win lay between Moss with the big Maserati, who was hot favourite, and Collins and Taruffi with the 4.1-litre Ferraris, while von Trips and de Portago were unknown quantities that needed watching. Likewise Gendebien with the Gran Turismo 3-litre needed watching closely, especially if there was any rain. In the big Gran Turismo class were many more 3-litre Ferraris and numerous 300SL Mercedes-Benz, but none driven by anyone capable of challenging Gendebien. At 5.30 a.m. on Sunday morning Scarlatti left, to lead the works cars, followed at one minute intervals by de Portago, von Trips, Herrmann, Collins, Taruffi then a break where Behra should have started, and finally Moss. As the

V8 Maserati roared out of Brescia to start the high-speed tour of Italy the crowds at the start returned home for breakfast. Already the rest of Italy was in a high state of excitement for the small cars were well on their way and the 750 c.c. Abarth-Fiats were approaching Rome. All along the route the roads were being closed about two hours before the first car was due, and back in Brescia they were being opened as soon as Moss had gone by.

As with so many Mille Miglias, this was not a Maserati day, for only 12 kilometres from the start Moss had the brake pedal break off at the root just as he was entering a fast bend. He managed to skitter round the corner but it was the end of the race for him and for Maserati, and the four Ferraris sped along the fast roads to Verona, Padova, Ferrara and the first control at Ravenna, little knowing that their chief rival

had already retired.
Weather conditions were ideal, with dry roads and light cloud obscuring the sun, so that the average to Ravenna was good, von Trips taking the shortest time of 1 hr. 37 min. 21 sec., an average of 186.748 k.p.h. Collins was second, Taruffi third, de Portago fourth and Gendebien fifth, so that already the race was turning into a Ferrari benefit. With competitors starting at one-minute intervals the position over Gendebien was interesting, for he had left Brescia at 4.17 a.m. as against the others in the Ferrari team who left after 5.30 a.m. as the Belgian was in the Gran Turismo class. This meant that he always arrived at controls long before the others, but until they clocked in it was not possible to gauge accurately his performance. With Moss out so early and Behra a non-starter, it was hoped that Herrmann would hold up Maserati fortunes, but just

before Ferrara he ran over a solid object and made a hole in the sump, so by the time everyone had gone through Ravenna the only hope for Maserati to get anywhere was Scarlatti in the 3-litre.

The Ferrari team received notification of only the first three positions at the Ravenna control, so that they did not realise that their only rivals were already out. The reactions to this monopoly were interesting, for von Trips eased up, Collins was shaken to have the German leading at the first control, so went much faster, and Taruffi, as always, really got into his stride down the fast leg of the Adriatic coast. Gendebien, of course, could know nothing of what was going on behind him,

and just drove as hard as he and the car could stand. By the time Pescara was reached both Collins and Taruffi had overtaken von Trips, and before they turned inland to head for Popoli and the mountains they realised the Maserati menace existed no longer, for Ferraris were still in the first five places. Scarlatti was doing his best, but he could form no challenge and he was just keeping ahead of Flockhart with the D-Type. Of the other large cars the American Chrysler Special had dropped out with a cracked brake drum and a split exhaust manifold, and Steed had retired with sticking brakes. Naturally there was much excitement in the other classes, but for the time being we must consider

those in the running for the out-right win. By Aquila the order was unchanged and the four sports Ferraris were conducting a clean sweep in the order Collins, Taruffi, von Trips and de Portago, with the Gran Turismo car of Gendebien ever in fifth place. Scarlatti was only just holding on to sixth place, for Maglioli with the Porsche was obviously going all out for a good position over all, rather than resting content with a certain class win, and he was already seventh, Flockhart having retired with the petrol tank adrift. Through Rome there was no change in the order and Collins now seemed certain of victory for there was no need for any of the Maranello drivers to force the

149

MILLE MIGLIA-ITALY-1,597 Kilometres-Conditions Ideal

* 1st: P. Taruffi (Ferrari 4.1 litre) 10 hr. 27 min. 47 sec. - 152.632 k.p.h.

2nd: W. von Trips (Ferrari 3.8-litre) 10 hr. 30 min. 48 sec.

* 3rd: Gendebien/J. Washer (Ferrari 250 GT) 10 hr. 35 min. 53 sec.

4th: G. Scarlatti (Maserati 300S) 11 hr. 00 min. 58 sec.

* 5th: U. Maglioli (Porsche 1,500 RS) 11 hr. 14 min. 07 sec.

6th: C. Luglio/U. Carli (Ferrari 250 GT) 11 hr. 26 min. 58 sec.

7th: "Ippocrate" (Ferrari 250 GT) 11 hr. 30 min. 55 sec.

* 8th: G. Munaron (Ferrari 500/TRC) 11 hr. 32 min. 04 sec.

9th: A. Buticchi (Ferrari 250 GT) 11 hr. 44 min. 27 sec.

10th: G. Koechert (Ferrari 500/TRC) 11 hr. 49 min. 02 sec.

11th: H. Schiller (Porsche Spyder) 11 hr. 54 min. 24 sec.

12th: S. Sbraci (Ferrari 500/TRC) 12 hr. 02 min. 08 sec.

13th: J. Guichet (Ferrari 500/TR) 12 hr. 08 min. 22 sec.

* 14th: P. Strahle/H. Linge (Porsche Carrera) 12 hr. 10 min. 08 sec.

301 starters, 163 finishers, 129 retirements, 9 unqualified.

CLASS RESULTS
Turismo and Gran Turismo

Up to 750 c.c.
1st: A. Thiele (Fiat Abarth) 13 hr. 32 min. 33 sec. - 117.925 k.p.h.

2nd: M. Guarnieri (Fiat Abarth) 13 hr. 38 min. 40 sec.

3rd: V. Gianni/L. Gianni (Fiat Abarth) 13 hr. 45 min. 57 sec.

750 c.c.-1,000 c.c.
1st: J.P. Vidilles (DB) 13 hr. 47 min. 42 sec. - 115.766 k.p.h.

2nd: P. Frere (Renault Dauphine) 13 hr. 47 min. 55 sec.

3rd: P. Garnache/H. Sellier (Renault Dauphine) 14 hr. 00 min. 20 sec.

1,000 c.c. to 1,300 c.c.
1st: R. Martin/M. Convert (Alfa-Romeo SV) 12 hr. 39 min. 44 sec. - 126.123 k.p.h.

2nd: P. Laureati (Alfa-Romeo SV) 12 hr. 44 min. 50 sec.

3rd: C. Spiliotakis/S. Zanonos (Alfa-Romeo) 12 hr. 48 min. 54 sec.

1,300 c.c.-1,600 c.c.
1st: P. Strahle/H. Linge (Porsche Carrera) 12 hr. 10 min. 08 sec. - 131.236 k.p.h.

2nd: D. Lissman (Porsche Carrera) 12 hr. 29 min. 45 sec.

3rd: H. Walter/H. Reinhold (Buick Carrera) 12 hr. 33 min. 18 sec.

1,600 c.c.-2,000 c.c.
1st: L. Nobile/P. Cagnana (Fiat 8V) 13 hr. 00 min. 49 sec. - 122.717 k.p.h.

2nd: J. Arosio (Alfa-Romeo Sprint) 13 hr. 18 min. 59 sec.

3rd: M. Travagini/L. Spina (Fiat 8V) 13 hr. 23 min. 54 sec.

Over 2,000 c.c.
1st: O. Gendebien/J. Washer (Ferrari 250GT) 10 hr. 35 min. 53 sec. - 150.688 k.p.h.

2nd: C. Luglio/U. Carli (Ferrari 250GT) 11 hr. 26 min. 58 sec.

3rd: "Ippocrate" (Ferrari 250GT) 11 hr. 30 min. 55 sec.

pace. The average to Rome was 172.965 k.p.h., so that it did not seem as though the leader was easing up at all. As far as the General Classification was concerned there seemed little likelihood of any changes and while the weather still remained good the speeds of the leaders remained high. On the fast winding stretches to Siena Collins continued to increase his lead and by Florence he was nearly nine minutes ahead of Taruffi. However over the Futa and Raticosa mountain passes the leading Ferrari began to make ominous noises from the back axle, and already Taruffi's car was showing similar symptoms, the extra power of the 4.1-litre engine presumably being too much for the transmission. Away from the Bologna control went Collins and Klementaski, both keeping their fingers crossed for the grinding from the back end was getting worse, and though they drove light-footed along the fast stretch to Piacenza they never made that city, for at Parma the grinding became too much and they came to rest with a broken rear axle. Meanwhile Taruffi had eased off a great deal, so that von Trips began to gain on him, and when Collins retired and Taruffi went into the lead the young German was running in

The Lancia Appia Zagato GTS of Enrico Anselmi, class winner of G.P. Nuvolari.
Bottom, the Triumph driven by Jean Morin reached Brescia after the final deadline.

company with the old man from Rome. Having started three minutes earlier it meant Taruffi had a certain lead of three minutes providing he kept his team-mate in sight. Behind them de Portago had slowed considerably and, unbeknown to him, Gendebien had passed into third place, for the Belgian was still pushing the Europa along absolutely flat out. Poor Scarlatti was completely on his own, but managing to hang on to his position, the Porsche being fast but not fast enough to beat a 3-litre Maserati.

When Taruffi went through Cremona with von Trips in close company it was obvious that they were touring in to win, both hoping that they would not suffer the same fate as Collins, while de Portago was now rather a long way back. Gendebien was first home of the works cars and an easy winner of the Gran Turismo class, but he had to wait until the others arrived to know his position overall. Taruffi and von Trips arrived back at Brescia run-

ning almost side by side, so that after being in the lead at some point or another almost every year in the past, but never finishing, Taruffi had at last finished a Mille Miglia, and to everyone's enjoyment he was the outright winner. Von Trips, making his first really serious drive for the Scuderia Ferrari, had more than justified expectations by finishing second.

After de Portago had gone through Cremona it was clear that he could not improve on Gendebien's time, so the Gran Turismo car was third overall, and it was just a matter of the Spanish driver getting to the finish, to be placed fourth. Alas, he never managed it for while travelling at close on 170 m.p.h. along a fast straight between Mantova and Brescia a tyre was said to have burst and the car was hurled into a ditch, to rebound across the road and into the opposite ditch, both driver and passenger being killed. This lamentable accident and the loss of two such keen sporting characters was a sad blow and caused the Mille Miglia to end on a rather unhappy note. Alphonse de Portago had been a truly sporting racing motorist; one with enormous courage, an ample share of skill and ability, and among the up and coming drivers of today; while his friend and navigator Edmund Nelson was a truly amateur sporting type

151

Sports Cars

Up to 750 c.c.

1st: G. Rigamonti (Osca) 13 hr. 20 min. 41 sec. - 118.342 k.p.h.

2nd: J. Laroche/R. Radix (Osca) 13 hr. 31 min. 11 sec.

3rd: G. Laureati (Osca) 13 hr. 40 min. 25 sec.

750 c.c.-1,100 c.c.

1st: G. Cabianca (Osca 950-c.c.) 12 hr. 51 min. 46 sec. - 124.156 k.p.h.

2nd: C. Manfredini (Osca) 13 hr. 22 min. 52 sec.

3rd: C. Falli (Osca) 13 hr. 32 min. 14 sec.

1,100 c.c.-1,500 c.c.

1st: U. Maglioli (Porsche RS) 11 hr. 14 min. 07 sec. - 142.141 k.p.h.

2nd: H. Schiller (Porsche Spyder) 11 hr. 54 min. 24 sec.

3rd: M. Saucken/G. Bialas (Porsche Spyder) 12 hr. 54 min. 05 sec.

1,500 c.c.-2,000 c.c.

1st: G. Munaron (Ferrari 500/TRC) 11 hr. 32 min. 04 sec. - 138.454 k.p.h.

2nd: G. Koechert (Ferrari 500/TRC) 11 hr. 49 min. 02 sec.

3rd: S. Sbraci (Ferrari 500/TRC) 12 hr. 02 min. 08 sec.

Over 2,000-c.c.

1st: P. Taruffi (Ferrari 4.1-litre) 10 hr. 27 min. 47 sec. - 152.632 k.p.h.

2nd: W. von Trips (Ferrari 3.8-litre) 10 hr. 30 min. 48 sec.

3rd: G. Scarlatti (Maserati 300S) 11 hr. 00 min. 58 sec.

"Coppa Nuvolari" Cremona-Brescia

1st: O. Gendebien/J. Washer (Ferrari 250GT) 39 min. 43 sec. - 199.413 k.p.h.

who went in these events for the sheer fun of the thing and a love of fast motoring, danger and excitement.

One by one the cars arrived back at Brescia, many suffering from mechanical troubles, many with bent and battered bodywork, but all who completed the 1,000 miles being justifiably well pleased with themselves, no matter whether they finished first or last, for 1,000 miles in a full day is good motoring by any standards and to cover that distance in anything between 10 and 16 hours is a worth-while feat.

In the foregoing discourse we have only dealt with the leaders on General Classification, but what of the rest of the 301 starters? Among the tiny cars that went off first, the Abarth-Fiats, with enlarged engines and pretty coupé bodies by Zagato, were making everyone blink, for these baby Gran Turismo cars were not hanging about. There was a close three-cornered battle between Thiele, Guarnieri and Gianni and in the opening stages their average was over 134 k.p.h. They soon caught the leading normal 600 Fiats, so that all round the course the thousands of spectators waiting for the first car to appear were surprised by these sleek little coupés whistling past like a group of angry bees. Thiele eventually pulled away from the other two, especially over the mountains, for his car was a works one and weighed quite a lot less than normal. It was this car that was first to arrive back at Brescia, having made the whole course at an overall average of 117.925 k.p.h., and though he was only 63rd in the complete picture, this class-winning speed was truly remarkable for a 750-c.c. car.

In the 750-1,000-c.c. touring and Gran Turismo class French cars dominated the entry and the works Dauphines had little opposition in the sub-division of the group. However, in the overall capacity group they were up against D.B. coupés, and though Vidilles won with a D.B. he was only seconds ahead of Frere in the Dauphine, who had been troubled with a slipping clutch in the early part of the race. Some indication of how the little Abarth 750 had gone can be gained by the fact that the larger-engined D.B. was 2 k.p.h. slower on average speed.

The 1,300-c.c. touring and Gran Turismo class was a complete walk-over for the Alfa-Romeo Giuliettas, the winners,

Right, the MGA of the Team Fitzwilliam of Carnegie, equipped with experimental disc brakes, finished fourth in class. Below, the Lotus XI of the Brescian Bruno Ferrari.

Martin/Convert, being 20th overall, amongst Ferrari, Maserati and Osca sports cars, but then the performance of the Sprint Veloce is no longer a thing that surprises. The surprise would be if they did not perform. Naturally there were dozens of these cars running, having pushed the 1,300 Porsche right out of the picture, and last year's Sprint Veloce Champion Eddio Gorza should have won easily but he retired after Pescara while well in the lead. Once the leading Giulietta had finished there came a seemingly never-ending stream of these beautiful little coupés, and in the final classification from

20th place onwards the name Alfa-Romeo appeared almost continuously. An equally fierce one-make battle was in the 1,300-1,600-c.c. class amongst a long row of Porsche Carreras and the regular Porschists Strahle and Linge dominated the scene with their very stripped Carrera, all superfluous weight having been removed, even to headlining and trim. In this general capacity class were the two works Sunbeam Rapiers, with engines enlarged to 1.5-litres, oversized fuel tanks and all the tuning mods. Unfortunately Miss Van Damm got a wheel in some particularly bad tramlines just

outside Verona and spun round, clouting a wall in the process. The other one, driven by Harper/Reece, went well apart from the throttle rod falling off at regular intervals, but was beaten in its class sub-division by a hot Ford Taunus from Germany.

The 750-c.c. sports class saw the usual collection of Italian home-made "specials", but it was the beautiful little Osca cars that dominated the class, in spite of opposition from works D.B. and Panhard. In the 1,600-2,000-c.c. touring and Gran Turismo class a remarkable number of DS19 Citroëns took part and ran like trains; it was veteran Chi-

ron who got the first one home, quite fast, but not fast enough to get near the 1,900 Alfa-Romeo saloon that won the class. Naturally enough the Gran Turismo 2-litres were even faster and a comparatively out-of-date 8V Fiat won this category.

The 750-1,100-c.c. sports class should have been a sort of super-club race amongst the Italians, with Osca, Ermini and Stanguellini cars, hot favourites being Morolli with a works Osca and Siracusa with a works Stanguellini. Unfortunately "the lads" were a bit put out when Cabianca took over the works 950-c.c. Osca after blowing up his 1,500-c.c. car the day before the race, for he was in a class of his own and simply walked away from everyone. It was most encouraging to see a pair of Loti running in this group, driven by Gregor Grant and Bruno Ferrari, the latter no relation to Enzo. It would have been quite something to have finished the 1,000 miles in a Lotus, but both fell by the wayside, Grant having trouble with a split fuel tank, and though he eventually limped back to Brescia it was not until everyone had gone home to bed. The 1,500-c.c. sports class was rather like the 1,100

The fortune also struck the Triumphs of Gottgens (right) and the courageous ladies' team of Nancy Mitchell and Pat Faichney (below) who were unable to repeat their feats of previous editions, retiring early in the race.

class, for there was no-one who could hope to challenge Maglioli with the works Porsche and he was so far out of the general run of his group that he figured prominently in the General Classification, being fifth overall and 40 minutes ahead of the next 1,500. In this class there was a fine display of M.G. MGAs and Carnegie, driving one of the Fitzwilliam team cars, was first home among the Abingdon contingent and fourth in the class, though this creditable effort also won him the class for sports-cars-that-cost-a-reasonable-price, a peculiar special category that ensures that a British car wins something.

Before the really fast cars left Brescia a small group went off consisting of touring saloons of more than 2,000-c.c., but with no holds barred on tuning or modification, and once more there was the nice sight of some opposition from England, there being a Ford Zephyr, driven by Riley/Meredith. Though it was hot as Zephyrs go the German cars were hotter and it could not keep up with the V8 B.M.W.s and 220a Mercedes-Benz; however, it was good to see someone from England having a go. The unlimited Gran Turismo class should have seen a good battle between Ferrari Europas and

Mercedes-Benz 300SL but Gendebien was unapproachable, being winner of the class by 50 min. and third overall, which was surely the most outstanding performance of the whole Mille Miglia. There were no SL drivers of great ability, but there were some good average runners and one of them should have finished second. As it was they all dropped out one by one and of the nine that started none of them finished, which was a black day for Stuttgart.

The 2-litre sports class looked like being a Maserati victory, for first of all Bordoni was well ahead, but he dropped out with gearbox trouble, then Bellucci took command until an oil pipe broke and finally Pagliarini went off the road and wrecked the front of his car. All this left Munaron comfortably in the lead with his Testa Rossa Ferrari, followed by the Austrian Koechert with a similar car. The big sports-car class we have already dealt with in discussing the General Category, and that too was not a Maserati day as we have seen. In the first 16 places of the whole race all but four were Ferrari cars, the four intruders being one Maserati and three Porsches, so we can truthfully say that the 1957 Mille Miglia was a Ferrari day.-D.S.J.

The victorious Ferrari 315 S (1) of Piero Taruffi crosses the finishing line for an average speed of 152.632 kph. Ferrari's triumph was completed by the second place of the 315 S driven by Wolfgang Von Trips (2), the winner of his category in the Nuvolari GP at an average speed of 197.178 kph. Olivier Gendebien and Jacques Washer, with their Ferrari 250 GT (3) finished third overall and won, their class, the GT category, the Index of Performance and the overall prize in the Nuvolari GP with an average speed of 199.412 kph. The only Maserati of over 2000 cc to finish was the 300 S (4) of Giorgio Scarlatti, fourth overall in front of the Porsche 550 RS (5) of Umberto Maglioli.

In the Turismo Preparato category the Saab 93 (1) of Lohmander and Krönegard won the 750 cc class, the Fiat 1100/103 TV (2) of Dino Faggi the 1300 class and the Peugeot 403 (4) of Guiraud and Chevron the 1600 class. The category was won overall by the Alfa Romeo 1900 TI of Achille Fona and Della Torre at an average speed of 114.548 kph. The category reserved for open sports cars with restricted retail prices was won by the Austin Healey 100 Six of Tom Wisdom and Winby (5).

In the Sport category the 750 class was won by the OSCA 750 (1) of Gian Carlo Rigamonti, beaten in the Nuvolari GP by the sister car driven by Jean Laroche and Remy Radix (2). Both prizes in the 1100 class were taken by the OSCA S 950 (3) of Giulio Cabianca. In the 2-litre class victory went to the Ferrari 500 TRC (4) of Gino Munaron, beaten in the Nuvolari GP by 500 TR (5) driven by Jean Guichet. Heinz Schiller (6) was the fastest of the 1500s on the Cremona-Brescia leg with an average speed of 181.152 kph.

The Turismo Speciale category saw the usual supremacy of the Renault 4CV 1063 with Louis Chardin (1) in the 750 class, and the Renault Dauphine (2) in the 1000 class with Paul Frère. In the 1300 cc class Roger De Lagneste won with the Peugeot 203 (3), whilst Ersilio Mandrini and Bertazzi won the 1150 cc sub-class with the Fiat 1100 TV (4), about half an hour behind the French car. The Ford Taunus 15 M (5) of J. Springer won the 1600 cc class.

1

3

2

4

5

1

The 2000 c class of the Turismo Speciale category was won by the Alfa Romeo 1900 TI (1) of Jean Aumas and W. Brandt, but overall victory in the category went to the BMW 502 (2) of A. Heuberger at an average speed of 123.710 kph. The Gran Turismo 750 class was won by the 750 Zagato (3) driven by Alfonso Thiele.

2

3

The 750 cc class of the Turismo Preparato, TS and GT group saw victory go to the Abarth 750 Zagato (1) of Marino Guarnieri, whist the 1000 cc class was won by the DB HBR (2) of Jean Claude Vidilles. The Alfa Romeo Giulietta SV (3) of Henry Martin and Raoul Convert won both prizes in the 1300 class.

1

2

3

The 1150 cc GT sub-class was won by the Lancia Appia GT Zagato (1) of Luciano Mantovani. Paul Ernst Strähle and Herbert Linge won the 1600 cc class with the Porsche Carrera (2). but were beaten by the sister car driven by D. Lissmann (3) in the Nuvolari GP. Luigi Nobile. along with P. Cagnana won the 2000 cc class and the relative Nuvolari GP with the Fiat 8V Zagato (4).

The Motor, may 22, 1957

EDITORIAL
REFORM NOT ABOLITION

The grievous loss of de Portago, one of the world's finest drivers, coupled with fatal injuries to a number of spectators, have inevitably led to a strong demand that the 1957 Mille Miglia should be the last of the 23 races which have been run from Brescia to Rome and back.

It is hard to balance the value of tradition against the loss of human life; it may seem inhuman to observe that drivers risk their lives at every race, and that a sensible number of the vast crowd of spectators watching the Mille Miglia would have met accidental deaths if they had been engaged on their normal daily life. Over-riding these arguments of pure reason is the undoubted fact that some measure of reform is a "political" necessity, although we hope earnestly that the race itself will continue on the calendar, even if it is run in different circumstances.

In 1940 the distance was covered on a triangular circuit some 100 miles in length, but to revert to this would change the whole character of the race and, if such a change be accepted, one might argue that it could then be better staged at Monza. Some may recall the expedient adopted in the pre-1903 Paris-Madrid town-to-town races, where competitors were controlled to a very modest speed through urban districts. The imposition of similar controls in Italy would present no technical difficulty, but if they covered every small village and township the effect would be somewhat farcical. Moreover, the danger of the cars getting out of control near a body of spectators massed between towns would still be present. A more sensible plan surely would be to confine competitions between the so-called sports cars capable of exceeding well over 150 m.p.h. to closed circuits, and to restrict the Mille Miglia to the Gran Turismo and Production categories. The very fast cars not only present the driver with difficulties in control but also have a kinetic energy 50% or more greater than vehicles with a maximum of, say, 140 m.p.h. Should they get out of controll they will therefore be liable to cause greater destruction.

On the other hand, if all the fastest cars had been excluded by regulations from the 1957 race, only the first four finishers out of 301 starters would have been eliminated and the winning average speed (by a Porsche) would have been 88.5 m.p.h., which is surely adequate to preserve the public spectacle. It may be argued that the connection between large-scale accidents and sports cars capable of Grand Prix performance is coincidental, but it would surely be better to continue racing with slightly slower cars rather than either to risk further loss of life or to abandon a race of long tradition which continues to command vast public interest.

EDITOR'S NOTE

The many names and datas reported may not correspond to the articles' texts, the General Classifications - both being reproduced as they were first published - and the captions. Moreover, in several cases our historical sources report drivers' names differently written. We list hereunder the names involved.

page 20	read Bosini	or	Bossini
pages 20, 77	read Maglioli	instead of	Magioli
page 23	read Maggiorelli	instead of	Magiorelli
page 52	read Kling	instead of	King
pages 58, 68, 132, 133	read Klemantaski		
page 61	read left	instead of	right
page 63	read Keen	insead of	Ken
page 65	read Halliwell	or	Helliwell
page 67	read Chidoni	or	Gidoni
"	read De Giuseppe	instead of	Guiseppe
"	read Goldani	or	Goldoni
page 68	read Presuzzi	or	Peruzzi
page 72	read Hengel	or	Engel
pages 72, 85	read Herrmann	instead of	Hermann
page 73	read Giletti	instead of	Gidletti
page 78	read Bratt	instead of	Brant
page 84	read Madrini	or	Mandrini
"	read Brancalion	instead of	Brancaleon
"	read Artesiani	instead of	Artesani
page 85	read Gignoux	or	Gagneaux
page 88	read kph 180.353	instead of	kph 182.306
page 91	read section	instead of	sectlegion
page 92	read Wolfgang	instead of	Wolgang
page 94	read Renauld	instead of	Renault
"	read Gatta	instead of	Gutta
pages 116, 145	read Denis	instead of	Dennis
page 131	read Boenson	or	Boësen
"	read Chiarel	or	Chianel
page 136	read Carrera	instead of	Carer
page 137	read Paolo Martoglio	instead of	Paolo
page 156	read (3)	instead of	(4)
page 158	read Lageneste	instead of	Lagneste
page 161	read Sträle	or	Sthräle

Finito di stampare
presso le Arti Grafiche D'Auria di Ascoli Piceno
nel mese di settembre 1998